With best wishes

John Ledger

26/06/2001

*Spirit*
OF THE
BUSH

# Spirit
## OF THE
## BUSH

MALCOLM AND PAUL FUNSTON
TEXT BY PETER BORCHERT

FERNWOOD
PRESS

**FERNWOOD PRESS**

P O Box 15344, Vlaeberg 8018, South Africa
Registration no. 90/04463/07

First published 2000

Edited by Leni Martin
Design (including map) and typesetting by Alix Korte
Production control by Abdul Latief (Bunny) Gallie
Repro co-ordinator Andrew de Kock
Reproduction by Unifoto (Pty) Ltd, Cape Town
Printed and bound by Tien Wah Press (Pte) Ltd, Singapore

ISBN 1 874950 28 8

*Dedication*

PHOTOGRAPHERS' DEDICATION
To our wives, Sue and Daleen

AUTHOR'S DEDICATION
To my children, who have so enriched my life:
Sarah, Caz, Simon, Nic and Tom

*Guineafowl scratch in the dust of mid-winter, amidst zebras, wildebeest, warthogs and a lone black-backed jackal.*

# Acknowledgements

## PHOTOGRAPHERS' ACKNOWLEDGEMENTS

A very special thanks to Peter Borchert who in his text has so eloquently captured the true mood and spirit of the bush. His profound knowledge of wildlife and his expert advice have proved to be invaluable and are deeply appreciated. Many thanks also to Pieter Struik whose vision, effort and enthusiasm have seen this book to completion. Leni Martin, as editor, and Alix Korte, as designer, have made an enormous contribution. For this, we are deeply indebted. We are most grateful for the contributions so eagerly offered by Eric Reisinger and Jamie Thom, and for all the kind help rendered by Gallo Images and by Max Fowles of Citylab, Durban.

We would also like to thank the following people for all that they have contributed to this book: Raymond and Dorette Bezuidenhout of Foto First, Nelspruit, for their invaluable assistance in acquiring equipment and with processing, and for their great friendship; Chris Johns and the National Geographic Society for support and encouragement, and a substantial film sponsorship; and Kruger National Park rangers Flip Nel, Louis Olivier, Kobus Kruger, Wikus van der Walt, Steven Whitfield and Scott Ronaldson for assistance and friendship during field research. Our friends in the Lowveld have also played an invaluable role, and we express our thanks to them: Harry and Rina Biggs, Robbie and Shirley Clark, Dewald and Annemarie Keet, Johann Knobel, Wayne and Inge Lotter, Gus and Margie Mills, Gordon and Marie Ramsden and Naas Steenkamp for wonderful times and constructive input.

**Malcolm and Paul Funston**

## AUTHOR'S ACKNOWLEDGEMENTS

During a long career in natural history publishing I have been privileged to meet many highly respected scientists who have shared their knowledge unstintingly. I have learned much from them and in the compilation of this text I have consulted so many of the books and articles they have written. To all of them my thanks, especially: Anthony Hall-Martin, Gus Mills, Ian Whyte and Ian Sinclair, Leo Braack, Piet van Wyk, Braam van Wyk, Ken Newman, Chris and Tilde Stuart, Bill Branch and Jonathon Kingdon. Among the numerous other works that are always to hand, I would like to pay tribute to *Sasol Birds of Southern Africa*, *Roberts' Birds of Southern Africa* and the *Sappi Tree-spotting Guide to the Lowveld*. I have not had the pleasure of meeting Richard Estes, but his *Safari Companion* is an extraordinary work that provides many insights into animal behaviour.

I would also like to thank Pieter Struik for his confidence in this project and for his support and patience while I laboured through the writing. I am proud to be part of a team with Malcolm and Paul Funston. Paul is an accomplished zoologist and I am most grateful to him for sharing his knowledge with me and for reading through the text and commenting on it.

As an editor myself, I know how important an editor is to a project of this nature, and I would like to thank Leni Martin for her sensitive and expert hand in shaping the final text. I would like to acknowledge, too, Alix Korte's talents that are so manifest in the design of this book, while Bunny Gallie, the production controller at Fernwood Press, also merits special mention.

**Peter Borchert**

**Left:** *'Brothers in arms' – two adult, fully maned, territorial male lions.*   **Above:** *A herd of buffalo mills around on a river bank.*

# Introduction

NOTHING IS DARKER THAN a moonless night in the African bush. Above, stars fill the sky with their pinpricks of light, an infinity of tiny sequins stitched onto the fabric of heaven's dome. But their brightness, reaching out over light years, is not enough to give even the vaguest form to the landscape. Instead, 'out there' the roar of a lion, the haunting cry of a jackal, the rumble of distant thunder speak of a primal state that seems little altered since well before our ancestors first walked upright and uttered words. To be in the bush on such a night is at once exhilarating and humbling; the great majesty of the universe is inspiring, yet also somewhat disquieting in the sense of one's own puny presence on this vast stage.

The desks of travel agents the world over abound with glossy brochures competing to entice people to visit Africa, waxing lyrical about the romance and mystery of the 'dark continent'. More often than not they are preoccupied with selling the 'big five' – lion, leopard, buffalo, elephant and rhino – and skim over, or even completely ignore, the smaller creatures that are equally fascinating. Yet, despite the hyperbole of the copywriter, there is an undeniable magic about Africa, especially its wild places where game moves more or less as it has done for countless centuries. Few of us fortunate to be in these places from time to time are not moved by the continent's great open spaces – it is a spiritual experience.

Carl Jung, the Swiss psychologist, always referred to Africa as God's country. In the autumn of 1925 he came to Africa and visited Kenya and Uganda, intent on learning something about the archetypal nature of mankind. During his East African sojourn, he woke at sunrise one day while travelling by train and on a steep red cliff he saw '… a slim brownish black figure standing motionless, leaning on a long spear'. It gave Jung an intense sense of *déjà vu*, prompting him to say: 'I could not guess what string within myself was plucked at the sight of that solitary dark hunter. I knew only that his world had been mine for countless millennia.'

Jung never came to South Africa, but there can be no doubt that his deep sense of the continent's spirituality and relevance for all humankind could only have been reinforced by the experience. Dr Ian Player, doyen of South African conservationists and himself a great follower of Jung, would undoubtedly agree. He puts it thus: 'I have seen the light of recognition come into the eyes of people from all over the world, as they have sat around a campfire with the sounds of Africa echoing in the darkness, or watching Scorpio rising, followed by the full mysterious moon. The Africa within, which we carry, sees the mirror image of the Africa without, and something within the soul responds. "I shall never be the same again" is a phrase so often used by those who come to Africa.'

In southern Africa there are many special places that evoke a sense of spiritual wonder: the Namib Desert and the wetlands of the Maputaland coast, the vast expanse of Etosha, the Okavango Delta, Table Mountain, Victoria Falls ... The list goes on, but it would not be complete without the inclusion of the far northeastern corner of South Africa where, forming a common boundary with Mozambique along a low ridge of mountains known as the Lebombos, lies one of the greatest conservation areas in all of Africa. This is the Lowveld bush, with the Kruger National Park as its focus – a vast tract of land, a full 350 kilometres from north to south and 90 kilometres across at its widest point. Some two million hectares in extent and South Africa's largest national park, it represents some 20 per cent of all conserved land in South Africa.

The status of the Kruger National Park is huge. It stuttered into life during the early decades of the 1900s and has matured through many vicissitudes to become without question one of the most renowned sanctuaries for wild animals in the world. The park deserves recognition as a World Heritage Site, and its importance as a tourist destination is paramount in South Africa's burgeoning ecotourism industry. Nearly one million visitors make the pilgrimage through its gates each year, generating an annual income for the park approaching R200 million.

This contribution to the country's economy is even greater when the private reserves that nestle at the western flank of the park are taken into account. Here, game lodges with enticing names like Mala Mala, Sabi Sabi, Londolozi, Ngala and Singita offer an experience of the bush that combines the height of luxury – outstanding setting, accommodation and cuisine – with exploring the wild in open Land Rovers under the guidance of attentive rangers. Wildlife encounters are often close-up, as the animals have become habituated to the vehicles and hardly react at their approach.

Such experiences may be reserved for the wealthy, but they make the experiences to be had in the adjacent national park no less special. What the Kruger Park may lack at the top end of the ecotourism market, it makes up for in many other ways. Whereas it is very appealing to be pampered in every respect, there is also

*A pair of saddle-billed storks on the lookout for fish in a fast-flowing stream.*

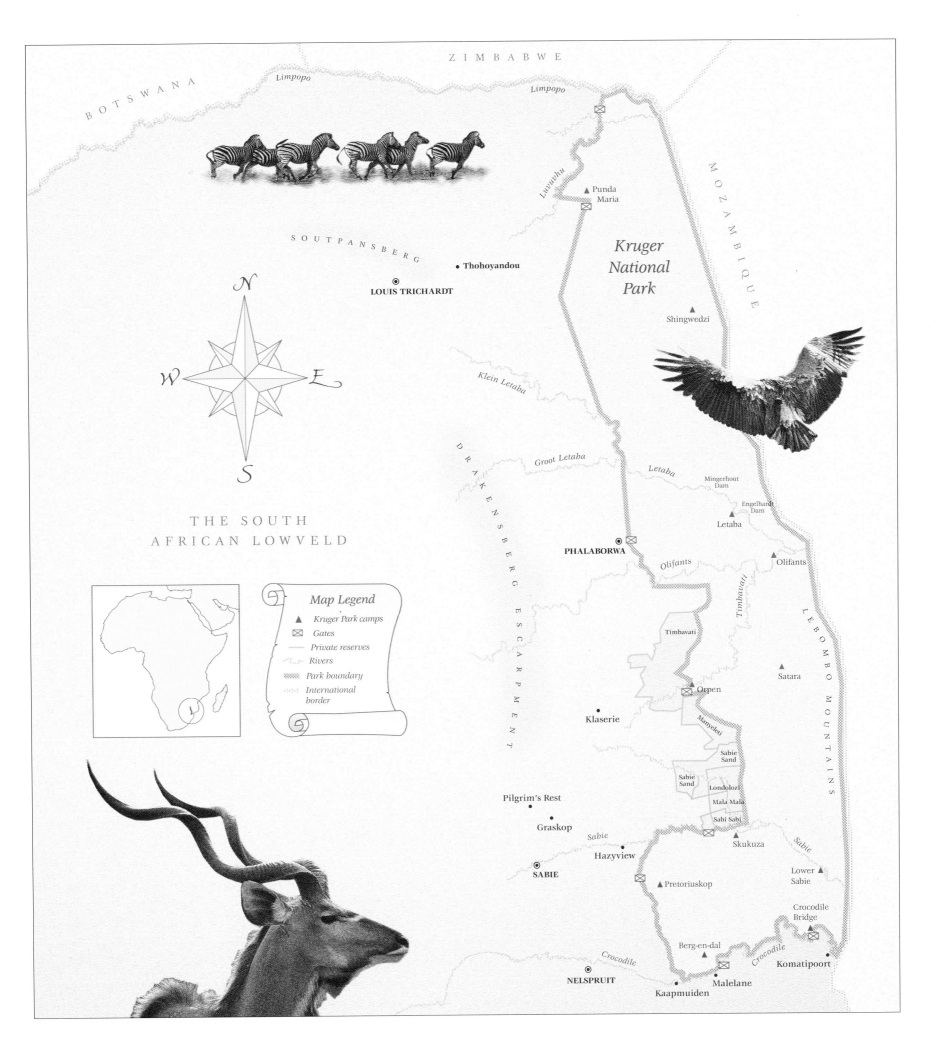

BOTSWANA

ZIMBABWE

*Limpopo*

*Limpopo*

M O Z A M B I Q U E

S O U T P A N S B E R G

*Luvuvhu*

▲ Punda
Maria

● Thohoyandou

*Kruger
National
Park*

◉ **LOUIS TRICHARDT**

▲ Shingwedzi

N

W      E

S

*Klein Letaba*

D
R
A
K
E
N
S
B
E
R
G
*Groot Letaba*

*Letaba*

Mingerhout
Dam

Engelhardt
Dam
▲

THE SOUTH
AFRICAN LOWVELD

E
S
C
A
R
P
M
E
N
T

▲ Letaba

◉✉ **PHALABORWA**

*Olifants*

▲ Olifants

L
E
B
O
M
B
O

*Timbavati*

*Map Legend*

▲ *Kruger Park camps*
✉ *Gates*
── *Private reserves*
〜 *Rivers*
▨ *Park boundary*
⋯ *International
border*

Timbavati

▲ Satara

M
O
U
N
T
A
I
N
S

✉ Orpen

● Klaserie

Manyeleti

Sabie
Sand

Sabie
Sand

Londolozi

Mala Mala

● Pilgrim's Rest

Sabi Sabi

✉

*Sabie*

▲ Skukuza

*Sabie*

● Graskop

● Hazyview

◉ **SABIE**

▲ Pretoriuskop

✉

Lower ▲
Sabie

Crocodile
Bridge

▲ Berg-en-dal

*Crocodile*

*Crocodile*

✉ Komatipoort

◉ **NELSPRUIT**

✉

● Kaapmuiden

Malelane

a very special pleasure in being able to cook one's own food over an open fire in the park camps. And even when out and about looking for game, it is somehow very satisfying to follow the roads in one's own vehicle and to encounter the animals by chance rather than to have them 'delivered'. Above all else, there is a sense of great space in the Kruger National Park.

The true foundation of the park, however, lies not only in its impressive size, but also in its extraordinary diversity of plant and animal species. Few, if any, of the world's other great national parks can match the number and variety of life forms that live here. For example, nearly 150 different mammals have been recorded: the big, impressive animals are all here – lion, leopard, cheetah, hyaena, wild dog, buffalo, elephant, rhino (both black and white), zebra, wildebeest, eland, kudu, sable, roan, nyala. And then there are the smaller mammals, from the gracile impalas that are everywhere to the tiny mice and gerbils that are also prolific but not always noticed. More than 500 bird species have been recorded, many of which are resident all through the year, but others come only for the summer months when food is plentiful. Other animal groups are also well represented: 114 reptile, 50 fish and 33 amphibian species are known. Plantlife, too, is rich and varied, from tropical to subtropical: almost 2000 species have been identified, including some 450 trees and shrubs, and 225 grasses.

In the eyes of many people, these statistics alone should guarantee the Kruger Park's survival in perpetuity. Yet, some 75 years after its proclamation, it faces challenges the like of which it has never before had to meet. These form a mesh of tightly interwoven social and economic threads that sometimes seem to defy unravelling: the park is an island flanked by impoverished rural communities, mines and, on the high escarpment that rises to the west, huge plantations of exotic timber. To the north and east respectively lie the countries of Zimbabwe and Mozambique, each with its own set of similar socio-economic dilemmas.

Six major rivers run through the Kruger Park or along its boundaries, but none of them rises there. Instead they begin to the west among the crags of the escarpment and, further afield, on the Highveld massif itself. On their seaward journey they pass through plantations, towns and rural settlements, farmlands and sites of mining and other industry. The people, their homes, crops and industries all need water to sustain themselves, and the demands on the rivers are great.

It may seem strange, in the early months of the year 2000, to be writing of 'water problems' when the Lowveld and neighbouring Mozambique and Zimbabwe have been inundated by the worst floods in living memory. But those who know the bush will also be mindful of the dry times when the wilderness has verged on dying of thirst. It is as well to remember that rainfall is at best erratic in southern Africa, with periods of extreme dryness alternating with extreme wet periods in irregular cycles.

These are not unique problems – in some form or another they face conservation areas the world over and are products of weather patterns, high population numbers and our overly consumptive societies. But it is not all doom and gloom, for in South Africa at least the tide seems to be turning. Innovative water-management policies; a growing awareness of wide-reaching environmental responsibility on the part of industry; the beginnings of a better understanding between conservation needs and human needs; and, at long last, a realisation that sound conservation and carefully managed tourism hold a major key to unlock the full economic potential of the land – these are all encouraging signs.

Perhaps one of the most exciting initiatives in securing the long-term conservation future of the Lowveld is that of the Peace Parks Foundation, which seeks to unite the Kruger National Park with conservation areas in Zimbabwe and Mozambique to form a transfrontier conservation area of some 95 000 square kilometres. The process, begun in 1997, is painstaking, but already there are signs of progress. What a victory for world conservation when this becomes a reality!

The economic benefits of formally linking these areas through inter-state agreement, common conservation objectives and local community support are many, but sometimes it is hard to fix the mind on such 'macro' matters when in the bush. Something else takes over, a something that, even if it remains unarticulated, is very close to the spirituality expressed in the words of Carl Jung and Ian Player. The rest of the world, with all its problems, recedes when you are in the Lowveld wilderness, and all that matters is the sense of space and the life, big and small, that surrounds you.

It is this 'spirit of the bush' that we have attempted to express in these pages.

**Right:** *A lone wildebeest bull splashes across a Lowveld river.*

1   *A detail of baobab bark.*
*Unlike other trees, baobabs*
*have the ability to regenerate*
*their bark, a useful attribute*
*considering the extensive*
*damage caused to these trees*
*by elephants.*
2   *A delicate baobab flower.*
3   *The large and hairy fruit of*
*the baobab has a velvety texture*
*and is yellowish grey, turning*
*to brown as it ripens during*
*April through May.*

**Above:** *The silhouette of a stately baobab towers above all else in the Lowveld landscape. It is an unmistakable tree, with its massive trunk and thick limbs that divide and spread to form a great canopy, bare in winter but clothed in deep green foliage from October through to May. The baobab prefers the deep, well-drained soils associated with alluvial plains and rocky areas, and is widespread throughout the Lowveld north of the Olifants River. It has strong links with wild animals – elephants are particularly fond of the bark – and humans traditionally cook the leaves as 'spinach', eat the fruits (the pulp of which is rich in vitamin C), use the leaves and bark as a remedy for treating malaria and dysentery, and even roast the seeds as a coffee substitute.*

# Living Sentinels

IF WE COULD TAP into the 'memories' of the giant baobabs of the Lowveld bush, what extraordinary things would we learn? Other trees may grow old and tall, each one undeniably adding to the beauty of the landscape, but baobabs are truly the living sentinels of the Lowveld. Some are known to have lived for 2000 years and more, and we can only wonder at their experience. They have witnessed the comings and goings of man and the passage of countless animals. They have survived the fires that periodically sweep through the veld, and have withstood repeated vandalism by elephants eager for their moisture-holding bark. A stately specimen like the one above may not have achieved the great age of others of its kind, but it has certainly stood guard atop 'Baobab Hill' for a very long time, a centuries-old landmark for all who have passed by.

Though much studied, the baobab does not yield its secrets easily. We may know that its flowers flourish and wilt within a day and that they are pollinated at night by bats attracted by their strong carrion odour. And we may know that the pulp of the fruit, rich in ascorbic, tartaric and citric acids, makes a refreshing drink; that the bulbs at the root terminals can be dried and ground to make a porridge; that the fruits, leaves and stems are a favourite food of elephants; and that almost alone amongst trees, baobabs have the remarkable ability to regenerate bark. But we have been unable to unravel much of the origins of baobabs, an ancient group of plants represented by only one species on the African continent, another in western Australia, and several on Madagascar.

Baobabs may seem permanent and indestructible, but they lack the hard wood of other tree species and when they do die they disintegrate into an untidy mass of tangled fibres. In what seems like no time at all, there is little or no evidence that once the site was graced by one of the most enigmatic trees ever to have inhabited the earth.

# Western Ramparts

ON THE SCALE of geological time, even the longest-lived baobabs are no more than the merest flashes of light on the retina of creation. The origins of the Lowveld landscapes as we know them today reach back through some 2000 million years to a time of seismic activity beyond imagining. Colossal outpourings of molten rock bore down on older rock strata, cooling to form a mantle so heavy that it caused the eastern rim to tip upwards, creating in the process the escarpment that has guarded the western border of the Lowveld to the present time. Much altered by the relentless erosive powers of wind and water, this eastern escarpment of the Drakensberg range – itself the southernmost extension of the Rift Valley system that transects Africa – is one of the scenic highlights of southern Africa. Deep, forested ravines and spectacular cascades and waterfalls are all part of the upland character. From certain vantage points, such as the aptly named God's Window, the land falls almost sheer for more than 1000 metres to the thick, steamy heat of the Lowveld below.

Scarcely more than a century ago there would have been little evidence here of modern man and certainly none of his mines, towns and plantations that disfigure the present-day landscape. Then the Lowveld stretched unscarred from the foot of the escarpment cliffs eastwards, over the low ridge of the Lebombo Mountains and on towards the coastal plain of Mozambique beyond.

The Lowveld of old must have been a forbidding place, infested with tsetse flies and malaria-bearing mosquitoes, and teeming with elephant, lion, buffalo and other wildlife. Now only remnants of that wildlife still exist, mostly within the protected areas of the Kruger National Park and surrounding reserves. Certainly the Lowveld was not a welcoming place, according to James Stevenson-Hamilton, that doughty and determined British soldier who gave so much of his life to the formation of the Kruger Park. He often spoke of its brooding spirit and, given a quiet, isolated spot and a reflective mood, that spirit can still be felt – a palpable sense of a wild, untamed place.

**Below:** *The sandstone cliffs of the Mpumalanga Drakensberg loom high over the landscape, separating the low-lying bush of the Lowveld and the high grasslands of the hinterland.*

**1** *Waterfalls are a feature of the Drakensberg escarpment, where many rivers tumble spectacularly through rocky gorges.*

**2** *A klipspringer casts a watchful eye over its surroundings from the relative safety of a high vantage point. Its vigilance is as much prompted by the possible intrusion of a rival into its territory as it is by the need to avoid the attentions of a predator.*

**3** *The beautifully marked five-lined or rainbow skink.*

1

2  3

# Arteries of Life

THE FIVE MAJOR RIVERS that flow through the Lowveld – six if you count the Limpopo, which touches the Kruger National Park along its northern boundary – are critically important to the region's ecosystems. Although the summer rains are often long and heavy, the Lowveld is not rich in water resources. No big rivers rise here, there are no lakes or other expanses of permanent water, and when the rains don't come, as happens from time to time and sometimes for several seasons in succession, then dryness and stress come to all living creatures with alarming speed.

It is hard to imagine such a scenario when the Sabie, Olifants, Letaba, Crocodile and Luvuvhu rivers are swollen and wide, when their tributaries roil and race, suddenly transformed from the dry, tree-lined depressions that mark their courses for much of the year, and when the landscape is dotted with countless shallow pans. But the spectre of drought is a constant companion, and at the end of a long, dry and dusty winter a tension grips the veld as every living thing waits for signs of the first rains.

The vulnerability of the Lowveld to a lack of the water it needs to maintain its natural diversity is sadly heightened by man's activities. The Luvuvhu River, for example, has so much of its water extracted for agriculture that it no longer flows throughout the year. The Letaba is similarly affected – two species of indigenous fishes are known to have disappeared as a result – and the Crocodile, far to the south, is no better off.

The mighty Olifants faces the worst problems of all. Its headwaters are near Witbank far to the west, where mine workings and heavy industry pollute the young river and its tributaries. It then flows through poor farming area where overgrazing causes valuable topsoil to be washed away. As a final insult, and just before it enters the Kruger Park, it is joined by the Selati bearing its load of effluent from the mines of nearby Phalaborwa.

Only the Sabie River, rising on the escarpment, is relatively better off. But even it has problems: exotic, invasive plants infest its banks along its early course, and in places its progress is choked by water lettuce.

1  2

*Right:* *A small mixed herd of impala and kudu gathers on the thickly wooded banks of the Luvuvhu River, some individuals drinking while others keep a wary eye out for approaching danger.*
**1** *The slow meanders of the Letaba River, well fed by summer rains.*
**2** *The saddle-billed stork is a resident species of the Lowveld where, either alone or in pairs, it forages in shallow waters.*

1  2

# The Coming of Man

**Below & 1:** *The Masorini Iron Age site near the Kruger National Park's Phalaborwa gate has been meticulously transformed into an Iron Age homestead. It is open to visitors and provides a wonderful insight into the daily lives of an early Bantu-speaking settlement in the Lowveld.*
**2** *The ruins and archaeological finds at the Tulamela site near Pafuri in the far north of the Kruger Park speak of a gold-trading civilisation closely linked to that of Great Zimbabwe.*

WHAT WE SEE TODAY as a pristine Lowveld landscape devoid of human presence other than that of the tourist briefly passing through is essentially a delusion. Until the modern age, with its artificially managed wildlife areas bordered by fences to keep people out and the animals in, man and the creatures of the savanna acted out their lives together.

In a past as distant as a million years ago, early man may well have hunted in the Lowveld, moving from one place to another in rhythm with the seasons and the natural migration of animals. What scenes would have greeted our forebears *Homo erectus* and *Homo sapiens rhodesiensis*? What animals would they have watched from some high vantage over a river valley? One of a number of elephant species, maybe, or a giant hartebeest? These creatures probably did exist, along with giant baboons, giant buffalo, a short-necked giraffe, a hyaena weighing more than 200 kilograms, and many other long-extinct species.

The record of man in the Kruger National Park is almost continuous from the Early Stone Age through the Late Iron Age to the present. Our knowledge of his existence there is constantly being added to from the findings of ongoing archaeological research.

The park has one of the best preserved and most extensive concentrations of Late Stone Age sites in all of Africa. The San (Bushmen), who occupied the Lowveld from about 40 000 years ago to AD 200, left a rich legacy of rock art that may be found in some 115 known shelters, most of which are concentrated in the southern areas.

The San were still there when the first of the Bantu-speaking people arrived from the north, but before long they disappeared, ousted by the more powerfully built invaders who had long mastered the principles of metallurgy and iron working.

Of successive waves of new arrivals, one group settled south of the Limpopo River in the northern reaches of present-day South Africa, including the Kruger National Park. Their coming marked a new era of economic, technological and political activities that brought them, eventually, into contact with Arab traders and, later, the Portuguese. Quite literally, this was South Africa's first 'golden age', for the economy of the time – which reached its peak of influence in the twelfth and thirteenth centuries – was clearly linked to the precious metal and to the civilisation of Great Zimbabwe to the north.

**3** *A display of typical Phalaborwa pottery at Masorini. The styles and designs – still in use today by local Sotho-speaking people – show simple, cut decorations and have changed little over the centuries.*
**4** *One of the many San rock art sites in the Kruger Park.*

# Now and Then

IT IS 5.30 AT SATARA CAMP, on a spring morning that still bears a hint of winter chill. The sun has broken the horizon, sending low shafts of soft light across the veld. Guineafowl and francolins have discharged their duty by waking the world, while a pearl-spotted owl shrieks its last performance before retiring for the day. You are filled with anticipation for the coming day of game-viewing, and it seems as if the entire expanse of the Lowveld is waiting just for you.

Then, a different chorus. Here and there at first, but rapidly gaining in volume, the dull throbbing of motor engines invades your reverie. You are not alone after all, and outside a whole camp-full of visitors are taking to their motorcars and beginning to jockey for position at the gate, waiting for it to be swung open so they can be let loose for a day's sightseeing.

Any irritation at being a participant in the 'grand prix' start to the morning dissipates as quickly as the traffic, however, for the Kruger National Park is a very big place indeed. It stretches some 350 kilometres from north to south and is about 90 kilometres across at its widest point. Bigger than Belgium or the State of Israel, it absorbs close on one million visitors a year with ease. And, unless you run into a pride of lions near one of the larger camps in the middle of a major holiday period – in which case you could find yourself in a road-clogging press of cars – you can wander the network of roads for hours on end, hardly seeing another vehicle.

Seen from the air, the well-treed camps are hardly visible, little more than tiny islands of development in the vast ocean of bush. From the 'capital' of Skukuza and the other major camps to an ever-expanding array of small private camps, they offer the visitor every creature comfort.

In its own way, the Lowveld, including the many private game reserves adjacent to the Kruger National Park, has witnessed unprecedented development over the last few decades. After all, it was only in 1927 that the first tourist vehicles made their way gingerly into the park along a small section of barely traversable gravel track. In those days there were no facilities and visitors were free to camp where they pleased. They also had to ensure their own safety by carrying firearms and by building protective 'bomas' around their tents! Just over a decade later, the first permanent tourist camps had been built, 10 000 cars had passed through the gates carrying some 40 000 visitors, and the Kruger National Park was well set on the path that has seen it become one of the major big game destinations of the world.

**Above:** *Game-viewing in a time past – intrepid visitors to the Kruger National Park in its formative years make their way down a bush track. Today there is a strictly enforced code that would land any owner of a convertible travelling with the hood down in serious trouble.*
**1** *Today, game-viewing from an open vehicle is allowed, not only in the private reserves, but now also in the Kruger Park in open-sided, canvas-hooded vehicles.*
**2** *Bridges over the major rivers of the Lowveld are a comparatively recent development. Prior to their construction, the pont was the only means of getting across.*

1

2

1  2

*Left:  In the early days of wildlife conservation in the Kruger National Park, donkeys were a major means of transport, used to carry supplies and building materials.*
**1**  *A platoon of game guards stands to attention.*
**2**  *Colonel Stevenson-Hamilton in later life. Of this extraordinary man Harry Wolhuter wrote: 'I look back on my long, and very interesting, association with him with undimmed pleasure; and no superior officer was more loyal, kind and considerate to his subordinates.'*

# Old Guard

CHARACTERS HAVE ABOUNDED in the history of the Lowveld and tales of the people who came to settle in the region, handed down through generations of storytelling, are filled with acts of hunting prowess and individual bravery. James Stevenson-Hamilton, founding warden of the Kruger Park, had many adventures during his long tenure, and in his writings he left graphic accounts not only of his own close encounters, but also those of his colleagues. Among these were the experiences of the venerable and highly experienced rangers, Mafuta Shabangu and Harry Wolhuter.

Shabangu – as Stevenson-Hamilton pieced together afterwards – had discovered a group of lions lying up for the day and decided to fire at a lioness. He only wounded her and then had to set out in pursuit as she fled. Soon exhausted, the wounded cat lay down, only to rush out at Shabangu when he made his appearance. In the resultant fray, Shabangu managed to stab the lioness to death, but not before a savage bite to his thigh had severed an artery. The doughty ranger managed to bind his wound and attempted to make his way back to camp, but the loss of blood was too much. He settled down to rest and died soon after. The lions returned that night. Although they dragged Shabangu's body some distance, they did not savage it any further and left it to be found the next day.

Harry Wolhuter, a great name in the formative years of the Kruger Park, had a similarly gruelling duel, but survived. Wolhuter, it transpired, was riding home from the Olifants River when he caught sight of what he took to be a reedbuck. He just had time to register that the animal was behaving strangely when a grown lion exploded out of the bush towards him. He turned his mount side on, thus avoiding the full brunt of the attack, but the impact of the lion hitting the horse caused Wolhuter to fall, literally into the jaws of a second lion. As he was being dragged off, he managed to unsheathe his hunting knife and deliver three desperate thrusts into the side and throat of the lion, wounding it mortally.

Despite his wounds, Wolhuter managed to climb a nearby tree. Just in time, for the first lion, having chased the horse in vain, returned and began to patrol around Wolhuter's tree. Luckily members of his team found the badly wounded ranger and helped him back to camp. From there he still had to suffer a three-day journey by horseback and then train to reach medical assistance in Barberton far to the south.

Some years later Wolhuter visited the original vendor of the knife in Britain in order to purchase another like it. The salesman praised the quality of the blade and Wolhuter agreed. 'I know it is a good knife, I once killed a lion with it.' 'Oh, yes,' the salesman rejoined, 'I am sure you could kill a lion with it – it will kill a sheep!'

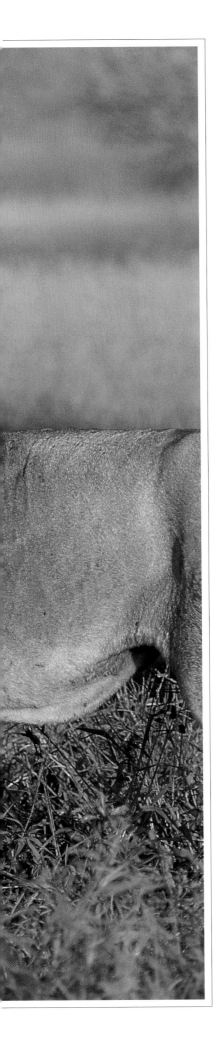

**Far left:** *A coalition of three mature lions at a kill. Such alliances are common in the social organisation of lions. The males are at their prime for a relatively brief period of between five and ten years, during which time an alliance will be dominant over several female prides in succession.*

**1** *The bond between coalition males is strong and continually reinforced.*
**2** *A lion exhibits 'flehmen', an open-mouthed stance during which air is drawn over a special gland which assesses the oestrus of a female.*
**3** *A lion pug mark in sharp relief.*

# United Fronts

IT IS A COMMONLY HELD NOTION that most lion prides comprise related females and their offspring under the 'protection' of a mature male. In reality, however, most prides are defended by coalitions of two or more males. These alliances sometimes form between related males of a similar age when they are evicted from their natal prides, but recent field research reveals that they also form between lions without common family ties. Of necessity, the coalition bond is very strong and intimate, for it is the key to the lions' ability to take over and hold a territory and the female pride it encompasses.

A coalition's association with a pride does not last for a particularly long period – on average no more than two to three years. This is long enough for the lions to mate with the pride females and to see the resultant cubs through to about two years of age, when they would be reasonably safe from other males. Then the coalition males usually desert the pride to seek out a new one. In this way the males gain considerably more reproductive opportunities in their lives than would be the case if they were to remain 'faithful' to a single pride.

The critical role of coalition males, therefore, is to create a safe environment in which the females can raise their cubs. This would be a virtually impossible task for a single male, especially in areas of relatively high lion density such as the Lowveld, for he would simply be chased out by an invading coalition. The newcomers would kill or evict defenceless pride cubs and then set about mating with the females to produce their own offspring.

The pride males diligently patrol their territories, constantly stopping to scent-mark and thereby set boundaries that rival males would cross at their peril. Central to territorial defence is roaring, which male lions do frequently throughout their border patrols, and with the utmost vigour. It appears, too, that the lions have a pretty accurate feel for their territorial boundaries, as they will charge towards other roaring lions if they suppose these rivals to be in or near their borders, but will ignore them if they are calling from well outside them.

**Below:** *Wild dogs are highly social animals and live in packs that range from a few to 20 or more adult members. Life centres around the breeding pair and their offspring. The puppies are born blind and helpless, and only emerge from the den after about a month.*
*1 Adults returning from a kill regurgitate meat for the puppies, now weaned off their mother's milk.*
*2 It is late afternoon, and the pack sets off to hunt.*
*3 A herd of zebras keeps a wary eye on a lone wild dog. The rest of the pack will not be far away.*

3

# Living in Packs

THE PHRASE 'GIVE A DOG a bad name...' could well have been coined for the African wild dog, for seldom has any animal been maligned and persecuted to such an extent. Dubbed a 'wanton and cruel killer that devours its prey while it is still alive, and a cannibal that will even attack and consume the sick and wounded of its own kind', it is little wonder that even today the wild dog is regarded with abhorrence by many.

Sadly, these often deeply rooted beliefs have no substance at all. In fact, recent field studies show that wild dogs have a highly complex social structure with a high degree of co-operation and caring among pack members. Moreover, of all the major predators, the wild dog is by far the most successful and efficient hunter, with some 85 per cent of pursuits ending in a kill. Hyaenas and lions trail abysmally by comparison, with only 20 to 40 per cent of their pursuits ending in success.

The African wild dog should be a very successful species – after all, it has the highest 'hit rate' of all the large carnivores and its hunting focuses on the large herbivores that are the most abundant. Why then is it in decline wherever it occurs in Africa? Only a few thousand exist and throughout its wide range it is endangered. The answer to this question is far from certain, but highly transmittable canine diseases such as distemper and rabies are thought to be responsible. Competition with other large carnivores, particularly lions, and even predation by them, are currently held as major reasons for the low relative numbers where wild dogs and their rivals co-exist.

Packs can comprise 20 or more dogs, but about ten is the average for the Kruger National Park and the surrounding reserves. Within the packs, which are usually made up of closely related males and females unrelated to them, there is a definite rank order, at the head of which is the breeding pair. Dominance is such that breeding is generally inhibited in subordinate members of the pack, and the only opportunity non-breeding females would have of procreation would be to emigrate and to chance upon a group of males.

Rank is a matter of some subtlety in a wild dog pack, for the dogs exhibit little of the vicious squabbling and fighting that is typical of other pack animals such as spotted hyaenas, lions and wolves. The principle strategy for avoiding aggression within the pack is the habit of begging, which characteristically takes place between pack members whenever there has been separation, or in the late afternoon after they rise from their midday siesta and prepare to go out hunting. This ritualised begging is also used by young dogs to get adult pack members to disgorge food for them to eat.

# Masters of the Water

HAULED OUT ON A SANDY SPIT or riverbank, a hippo can appear fat, lazy and ungainly. Only the inexperienced would be taken in, however, as on land this massive, grey, frequently grumpy and dangerous amphibian can move with surprising speed on its stubby legs. But it is in water that the hippo really comes into its own, for it is a powerful and disconcertingly fast swimmer. If we could submerge in clear water near a pod of hippos we would witness some extraordinary sights. Beneath the river surface they are agility personified, whether charging at speed – literally an underwater 'gallop' – or walking along the bottom, leaving the river floor and landing again with the slow-motion grace of moon-walking astronauts.

Hippos have been described as 'socially schizo-phrenic'. When they come ashore to graze at night, they do so independently. However, in the water, where they spend much of their day to escape the sun that would otherwise dry and crack their sensitive skin, and even while resting up on land, they live cheek by jowl. This high tolerance for close contact could be for the benefit of the calves, affording them protection from crocodiles, but it has also been suggested that the hippo's gregarious habits may simply be a strategy to accommodate the maximum number of animals in the space available. If calves are meant to be the prime beneficiaries, however, then there is also a downside. Although crowding must be effective against croco-diles, there is also the very real danger of the young-sters being crushed and trampled by their elders.

The only challenge to the hippo's dominion over the watercourses and pools of the African bush comes from the Nile crocodile. Mature adults typically reach three metres in length, or more; massive individuals of almost six metres and weighing more than 1000 kilo-grams have been recorded. Certainly, if time on earth were the only criterion for such mastery, the crocodile would win hands down, for this extraordinary reptile has been around, largely unaltered, for some 65 million years. It, together with other crocodile species – the alligators and the gharial of India – are all that remain of the archosaurs, which dominated the earth for some 150 million years, reaching their heyday during the Jurassic era 190 to 130 million years ago.

1

*1 The darter is often seen at Lowveld water bodies, showing a preference for quiet backwaters, pans and dams. It feeds mainly on fish but will also take frogs and insects.*

**Above:** *A pod of hippos lies hauled out on a boulder. Such basking is common, but the hippo generally avoids the worst heat of the day by retreating into the cool river pools. Its skin is especially sensitive to the sun's rays and often exudes a reddish, blood-like fluid. The function of this secretion is not properly understood, but it may act as a sealant against water loss.*
*2 A crocodile hunts in a shallow rapid. Large crocodiles of four metres or longer are able to subdue almost any unsuspecting animal at the water's edge, even buffalo.*
*3 A hippo 'yawns'. These displays are the opening gambit in territorial contests and are often made by young males advertising their willingness to fight.*

2　3

# Misty Morning

WITH THE COMING OF AUTUMN, the steamy Lowveld nights that give little relief after the enervating heat of a summer's day give way to a freshness that can descend to a biting chill. The comfort of a down-filled duvet or sleeping bag makes it a little harder, perhaps, to feel enthusiastic about an early morning game drive or walk. But a pullover and the fortifying pleasure of a hot mug of coffee or tea can do much to restore one's resolve to join the waiting game drive.

From a convenient vantage point all is quiet and, as if throwing down a silent challenge to the warming rays of the rising sun, a thick mist clings stubbornly to the low-lying land leading down to the river. Only the crowns of tall water berry, pod mahogany and lead-wood trees poke through to hint at the waters of the Olifants moving quietly by, hidden beneath this damp blanket. Even the animals seem a little reluctant to move about in the chilly air. But patience is rewarded when a lone elephant bull with heavy ivory lumbers out of the mist and begins to uproot great tufts of grass with his trunk, swiping them vigorously from side to side to remove clods of earth before raising the food to his mouth. A little way off, two hyaenas lope into view, mull about while sniffing at the air and then, with renewed purpose, set off at a fair pace and are soon lost from sight.

Slowly the day begins to warm and the sun beats back the mist to reveal the golden tones of autumnal Lowveld. In a nearby monkey thorn, now bereft of its foliage and all but a few of its purplish brown pods, a party of white-backed vultures begin to stretch their wings. Soon the rising warmth will generate the thermals they need to climb to their holding patterns high above the veld.

1

2

**Right:** *Two spotted hyaenas in a grassy clearing. The detail of their form is softened by early morning light filtering through the mist that lies over the land, cloaking it in an eerie silence broken only by the occasional call of an animal. Such misty mornings are common in the Lowveld, especially as autumn moves slowly to winter.*

**1** *A line of trees along a river bank fades into the thick mist rising from the water.*
**2** *The only solid figure in the muted light, a large bull elephant moves silently through the bush.*
**3** *A spider web glistens with droplets of moisture.*

3

1   2

3 4

# Dawn Chorus

THE FAR-OFF RUMBLE of a lion's roar seems almost gentle and benign as it reaches out through the darkness before dawn. Closer by, the long drawn-out *nyaaaa...* followed by a chattering *ya-ya-ya-ya-ya* heralds the presence of at least one black-backed jackal. A muted *prrrup prrrup...* A frog, maybe, or an insect? No, it is the call of a tiny scops owl. Its cousin, the wood owl, hoots softly from thick riverine bush, while a fork-tailed drongo begins its relentless scolding chatter.

The sounds are muted and intermittent. It is as if an orchestral movement on a vast natural scale is drawing to a slow, quiet close.

Suddenly the tempo changes. A short, harsh crowing starts up. Hesitant at first, then seeming to gain confidence, it quickly becomes louder and more persistent. Soon the air is ringing with the strident reveille of a Swainson's francolin. It, like the equally coarse cackling of the helmeted guineafowl, is a call to arms for the day shift. A woodland kingfisher joins in with a high, staccato entry note followed by a descending trill, and in no time at all it is as though every bird in creation is making its contribution.

The bush is alive with song, and with fleeting glimpses of small birds darting and flitting through the trees. Every now and then an individual call can be discerned – the burble of a coucal, perhaps, or the liquid piping of a black-headed oriole – but then it is lost again in the raucous chatter of red-billed woodhoopoes and the general confusion of sounds that make up the Lowveld's 'dawn chorus'.

The theatre of the waking day is one of the most exhilarating experiences in the bush. And all you need to do is sit quietly and wait for the performance to come to you.

# A Confusion of Stripes

THE ZEBRA 'GREW STRIPY' from hiding in the 'stripy, speckly, patchy-blatchy shadows' of a great forest, according to the *Just So Stories* of Rudyard Kipling. This is, perhaps, as good an explanation as any. For as much as the enigma surrounding the purpose of a zebra's stripes has been probed by animal behavioural scientists, none would be bold enough to state categorically why the essentially white coats of African horses should be as strikingly marked as they are with bold black bands.

There may not be a simple, straightforward answer, but scientists can hardly be faulted for a lack of plausible explanations. The stripes make it easy for zebras in a herd to locate one another; they create an irregular and moving pattern of light and dark which confuses predators, not allowing them to fix on a single target; or they baffle the flies that plague these animals of the plains. There is also support for the assertion that the stripes may serve a thermoregulatory function.

It has even been suggested that stripes help to minimise conflict among zebras. This possibility is the offering of no less an authority than the renowned mammalogist, Jonathan Kingdon. He maintains that young foals are constantly presented with a flickering pattern of stripes and associate this with the comfort and pleasure of the nuzzling and nibbling of their mother. In later life grooming becomes less frequent – zebras simply don't have time for it because of the constant need to graze (for up to 19 hours a day) – but they continue to make brief biting and rubbing motions in the air without actually coming into contact with one another. This may be a response to the ever-changing pattern of stripes in the herd, which they continue to associate with the pleasure of a mother's nibbling. Kingdon suggests that the stripes have a calming effect by 'switching off' aggression that would otherwise be more prevalent in close herding situations.

There probably is no single explanation, but scientists do agree that zebras have had their stripes for millions of years. Stone-age paintings in Europe suggest that early horses, which probably descended from zebras, also wore stripes. And so, rather than a zebra being a horse in pyjamas, it could well be that a horse is a zebra that has lost its stripes!

**Right:** *Two zebra stallions bite and kick each other in a contest for dominance over a harem.*

**1** *Burchell's zebra is the only zebra found in the Lowveld, where it occurs widely. It is most abundant, however, on the eastern savanna plains south of the Letaba River. Zebra are gregarious animals and are commonly seen in herds of five to 30 individuals (sometimes more), often in association with blue wildebeest.*

**2** *From a distance, all zebras seem identical, but closer inspection reveals patterns in their stripes that are markedly different from one individual to the next. Various theories as to the purpose of a zebra's stripes have been postulated, but it is unlikely that there is a single explanation.*

# The Bearded Antelope

MORE THAN ANY OTHER ANTELOPE, the blue wildebeest with its long shaggy beard and characteristic rocking-horse gait is synonymous with the African savanna. This fact, however, probably has more to do with its immortalisation in countless wildlife films about the Serengeti than with its existence elsewhere in the southern, central and eastern regions of the continent. And understandably so, as once seen in real life or on film, who could not gape in wonder at the vast herds numbering more than a million beasts moving with singular purpose across the landscape. Elsewhere in Africa there are still migrations of wildebeest, but none as spectacular and dramatic as that of the Serengeti.

In many parts of its range, the wildebeest's instinct to migrate towards greener pastures at the onset of the dry season is thwarted by the man-made barriers of fences, agriculture and general human developments. Sadly, the South African Lowveld falls into this last category and here the wildebeest, though relatively populous, is largely sedentary.

For most of the year wildebeest live in largely female herds comprising cows and their offspring of the previous season – on average about 30 individuals. These herds range within an established network of territorial males. Non-breeding males live in bachelor herds on the outskirts of these territories, often in less productive habitat. During the annual rut, which coincides with the onset of the dry season, the territorial males begin to round up the female herds and contests between the otherwise tolerant males reach a climax. With much noise – the croaking call has been likened to that of a giant frog – contesting bulls confront one another, dropping to their knees to spar if neither will give way. Once mating has taken place, and from then on well into the dry season, levels of territoriality again diminish, almost to the point of non-existence.

Gestation is about eight-and-a-half months and most calves are born within a three-week period soon after the onset of the summer rains, when the flush of green grass is at its most intense. The synchronisation of many births ensures the survival of some by providing a glut for predators. Furthermore, wildebeest calves are amongst the most precocious of all ungulates, and within a few minutes of birth are able to stand. After no more than two days they can keep up with the adults, thereby allowing migratory herds to retain their mobility.

*Above: A mixed herd of blue wildebeest and Burchell's zebra. Like zebra, the wildebeest of the Lowveld prefer open, grassy plains where they generally live in small herds, although sometimes they congregate in numbers exceeding a hundred. Wildebeest are among the favourite prey animals of lions, and each year thousands are killed by the powerful predators.*

*1 A female wildebeest with her offspring. A single calf is born to the female following an eight-and-a-half month gestation.*

1

# Ever-present Impala

IT IS NIGHT IN THE BUSH, with little light issuing from the sliver of a new moon. The ranger takes the vehicle's spotlight and slowly sweeps the middle distance, seeking out reflections off an animal's eyes. The probing beam picks out trees, rocks, termite mounds, throwing them momentarily into sharp relief, their detail heightened by the surrounding darkness. But no tell-tale pinpricks of light. Nothing. Then, suddenly, it is as though the power has been switched on in some small town. Hundreds of lights flicker in the distance. 'Impala,' the ranger explains and, as the light fixes briefly on the scene, it becomes evident that the lights of the 'village' are really the eyes of a large herd of grazing impala. Night or day, this is a common sight in the Lowveld, where impala are by far the most populous antelope.

If the leopard is the epitome of grace among the predators, then surely the impala commands this title amongst the hunted. Often overlooked because of its abundance, this beautiful, medium-sized antelope is worth watching, not only for its sleek, shiny-coated appearance, but also for the interaction between members of the herd. The interplay is constant, with individuals moving slowly through the veld as they crop the grass, pausing frequently to stare fixedly in the direction of some real or imagined danger, or to indulge in the ritual of grooming one another.

Sooner or later, however, one of the impala will lose its nerve and head off at speed. The effect on the rest of the herd is instantaneous: the peaceful grazing scene explodes in a confusion of bodies springing in every direction. It is a spectacular sight, as impala are prodigious jumpers, clearing as much as 11 metres in a single leap. It is also an effective defence strategy, especially against predators such as leopards that stalk to within pouncing distance.

At the end of the rainy season, impala society undergoes a stormy change as the normally peaceful herds are transformed by the brief annual rut. Males, usually tolerant of each other, begin to defend territories with great vigour and purpose. Any challenge to a territory evokes instant response, with much snorting, chasing and clashing of horns. It is an exhausting time for territorial males defending their right to mate with the females in their domains, and they have little time for grazing. By the end of the rut they have visibly lost condition, but their line of succession is assured.

**Above:** *Without doubt, impala are the most numerous of the antelope of the Lowveld, often congregating in sizeable herds. In the Kruger Park alone, where they frequently fall prey to all the larger carnivores, estimates of their numbers exceed 100 000.*
**1** *Only the male impala is horned. Here a mature male, displaying his long, double-curved horns to good effect, drinks at a waterhole, well attended by red-billed oxpeckers gleaning ticks and other parasites.*

2 Impala males indulge in a mutual grooming session.
3 Any tolerance displayed between mature males, however, comes to an abrupt end in the presence of females in oestrus and at the time of the annual rut at the end of the rainy season. Combat is the order of the day, and the characteristic snorting roars and clashing horns resound through the bush as males engage in serious contests for dominance over a herd of females.

# Smaller Antelopes

IT'S OFTEN JUST A FLICK of an ear that attracts one's attention to the tiny, reddish brown antelope standing stock-still, all but perfectly camouflaged in the tall, golden grass of early winter. For a moment it stares back, and its large, prettily marked ears – far too big for such a petite creature – fix in your direction. Then, as if suddenly losing its nerve, the little steenbok turns and in a few darting leaps is absorbed back into the veld.

The steenbok is one of the more frequently seen of the 'dwarf' antelopes that include Sharpe's grysbok and the common or grey duiker, primarily because it tends to spend more time in the open whereas the other species are secretive, hiding up in wooded areas.

Not much is known about the private lives of the smaller antelopes, as they have been poorly studied. Unlike the great herds that characterise the society of many of the larger antelopes, however, the smaller species live out their adult years as monogamous pairs. And, even though these couples share and vigorously defend the same territory, they tend to forage, hide and rest up singly.

Probably the best known of the smaller antelopes is the compact klipspringer, which is frequently seen perched on some high, rocky promontory. The klipspringer – literally translated, it means 'rock jumper' – is aptly named, as it is extremely agile and leaps with balletic grace from boulder to boulder, taking off and landing on the tips of its hooves. This agility enables the klipspringer to exploit the moisture- and nutrient-rich vegetation found on eroding cliffs and hillsides, areas that are not accessible to other browsing antelope. In fact, its greatest source of competition for food probably comes from the ubiquitous rock hyrax, or dassie, that greatly outnumbers it through its range.

1

*Right: A male bushbuck stands among the leaf litter in a woodland clearing. As their name suggests, bushbuck are seldom seen any distance from the thickly wooded areas fringing rivers and permanent waterholes.*
*1 A female steenbok lying up. The branching pattern in her large, cupped ears is diagnostic.*
*2 A pair of klipspringers browse at the base of 'their' koppie.*
*3 A common, or grey, duiker browses in thick, verdant bush. Duikers are also well adapted to times of drought as they derive their moisture needs from their food.*

2    3

**1 & 2** *Luxury accommodation in chalets, all discreetly out of the line of sight of one another, is one of the hallmarks of the exclusive private game lodges that cluster along the western boundary of the Kruger National Park. Combining the 'bush experience' with the superb food and pampering comfort associated with top city hotels is the special talent of lodge owners.*

# In the Lap of Luxury

IMAGINE THE SCENE... You and a few other guests are seated in an open Land Rover bumping and grinding its way along a baffling network of switchback paths through the bush. Ages ago you lost any sense of direction you may have had. But who cares, for at the helm is a young man – or, these days, a young woman – completely at ease, exuding charm and, in most instances, exceptionally well tutored in the ways of the wild. Furthermore, a rifle lies comfortably in its housing on the dashboard and, perched on a jump seat on the bonnet or on the rear seat of the vehicle, is an experienced tracker. You're in good hands and you know it. After all, your guides have just spotted fresh lion spoor crossing the track and now you're in hot pursuit. Broken exchanges over the radio, with much crackling and hissing, take place between your ranger and one of his colleagues elsewhere on the property.

It's getting dark, but no matter, for the vehicle is armed with a million-candle-power spotlight expertly wielded by your tracker. Then, around another couple of turns, the light catches the pride. A wildebeest has been brought down and you have arrived on your movable grandstand to witness the feast.

Later, after maybe an elephant sighting or two, a glimpse of a leopard disappearing into thick riverine foliage, and several smaller creatures such as scrub hares, genets and bushbabies caught momentarily in the fierce glare of the spotlight, you arrive back at the lodge. A superb meal awaits, probably in an open, reed-walled 'boma', and a chalet dressed with furnishings that speak of the ultimate in comfort and luxury will be your palace for the night.

This is the experience to be had at any one of the many private game lodges that hug the western flank of the Kruger National Park. There are subtle differences between them, of course, and some are definitely better than others, but generally the standard of the lodges and the game-viewing are exceptionally high, with sightings of the 'big five' being as assured as they could be.

**Above:** *A game drive in a 4x4 vehicle in the company of a well-informed ranger and an armed guard is at the very heart of a stay at a private game lodge. The animals have become habituated to the vehicles and perceive them as non-threatening. They see the vehicle as a whole and do not distinguish individual humans, who are cautioned not to stand for a better view, thereby breaking the outline of the vehicle.*
**3** *Birdwatching from the comfort of a lodge deck.*
**4** *A typical private game lodge spread along the shoreline of a waterway.*

3    4

# Close Encounters

TO THE UNTRAINED EYE there are no signs, no clues to what has passed this way and when. No path is visible in the tall grass. But the ranger up ahead has seen something and he motions the group in his charge to keep down and come closer. It's not much, but he points low down to a tuft of darkish fur caught on the vicious snares of a small wag-'n-bietjie thorn tree. 'Cheetah,' he whispers. The force of the snagging thorns grabbing at the animal's coat has split the thin twig, but not broken it. The wound is still moist, so evidently recent. Slowly the party moves forward; suddenly the ranger pauses again and points ahead and to his left. There, no more than 20 or so metres away, is a cheetah standing on the low rise of a termite mound. She is facing away, intent on something or maybe just casting about from her vantage. But then she is aware of her pursuers. The beautiful head, with its characteristic 'tear marks' clearly visible, snaps round to stare momentarily and then, in an instant, she is gone...

Encounters such as this are exhilarating in the extreme. It is one thing to see wild animals close up from the safety of a vehicle; quite another to come across them on foot. Suddenly you are on their turf and they have the advantage.

Although one sets off hoping to come across one of the big game animals while walking in the bush, the experience becomes so much more than just that. The smaller creatures – the spiders, insects and maybe the odd rodent – are suddenly in sharp focus. The birds are all around you instead of just in front, and you see close up the true beauty of a small flower, a drop of dew on a web, and the delicate structure of a discarded feather. Quickly you learn to watch where you place your feet so as not to destroy a pug mark or hoof print in the sand.

And more than anything else, you learn what most of us have never known in our cloistered city environments. There is a sense of discovery about ourselves and where we come from, a sense of rekindling skills lost many generations ago and, especially as night draws in, a sense of place. To walk in the African bush is to enrich the soul, and a rare privilege indeed.

*Above: Experiencing the bush close-up, on foot, is rewarding beyond expectation, especially in the company of a well-trained guide eager to share his intimate knowledge of the veld and its lore. While walking safaris in the Lowveld can, and often do, include close encounters with big game, these are chance happenings. What is guaranteed is a lasting memory of the smells of the bush and learning to identify spoor and other signs of the wild, as well as the trees, birds and smaller creatures and plants that are so often overlooked from a vehicle.*

*1 A tree squirrel pauses briefly in its quest for food, which includes flowers, leaves, wild fruits and insects.*
*2 A false tiger moth displays its vivid coloration.*
*3 An eastern tiger snake.*
*4 A caterpillar of the family Noctuidae inches its way along a grass stem.*
*5 An armoured ground cricket.*

4

5

# Birds, Birds and More Birds

A DEEP, RESONANT *OOOMP* floats across the stillness, and then another and another, until it sounds as if there is a small flotilla of tugboats communicating their way through the early morning mist. Ships in the bush? Impossible. Then a huge black bird emerges purposefully from the tall grass into a small clearing and several companions follow. No one could call them pretty, with their bare, scarlet faces, equally red, bulbous throat pouches and massive down-turned bills. More booming, and it is evident that the calls are coming from these ground hornbills 'talking' to one another as they stride through the veld, feeding on any small creature they encounter.

Even if you wanted to, you could not escape the sounds of birds. Whether the lonely *du, du, du, du...* of an emerald-spotted dove, the cry of a fish eagle or the harsh cackle of a marauding band of arrow-marked babblers passing through a camp, they are all around. There are more than 500 species of birds in the Lowveld, some rare or just visiting in the summer months, but most familiar and resident throughout the year. Not surprisingly, the Kruger National Park and surrounding conservation areas are high on the list of favourite destinations for avid bird lovers.

That some 50 per cent of all the birds found in southern Africa live in, or at least visit, the Lowveld is no accident. There are 35 recognised landscape types, with over a dozen distinct habitat types ranging from rivers and ephemeral streams and pans, through sandveld and mopane forest, to thornveld and patches of open savanna. Contributing, too, is the fact that the northern parts of the region extend into the Limpopo River basin where a number of species reach the southernmost limit of their distribution. Around Pafuri, which is easily reached from the Punda Maria and Shingwedzi camps, sightings of long-tailed starling, three-banded courser or racket-tailed roller, for example, could well reward the vigilant.

**Far right:** *An African spoonbill picks its way through the shallows. It forages for small fish and aquatic invertebrates by sweeping its spatulate bill, partly or completely submerged, from side to side. Sometimes it will also probe the mud to find food.*

**1** *The glossy starling is a common resident of the Lowveld. A master opportunist, it is almost always present at camps and picnic sites, taking advantage of rich pickings.*

**2** *A pair of painted snipe forage along the periphery of a reedbed. Somewhat nomadic in habit, painted snipe are not often seen in the Lowveld.*

**3** *A lilac-breasted roller firmly grasps its insect prey.*

**Left:** *The leopard's adaptability to a wide range of habitats is a key element in its survival.*
**1** *Leopards can survive long periods without water, but drink when they have the opportunity.*
**2** *A leopard cub.*
**3** *A leopard hauls a warthog carcass into a tree. Such 'lardering' is an important tactic in preventing a kill from being commandeered by competitors such as lions or spotted hyaenas.*

# The Ultimate Cat

ALMOST ALL DESCRIPTIONS of leopards extol the cat's virtues as a creature of rare grace and beauty, the Prince of Stealth. Though they sometimes border on hyperbole, it is difficult to fault these verbal attempts to capture the essence of this enigmatic carnivore. No other African cat – not even the lion – evokes such a response in humans. Indeed, the leopard is, as one commentator has described, 'the embodiment of feline beauty, power and stealth'. More than this, perhaps, it is the aura of mystery surrounding the leopard that fires our imagination.

Man has known leopards since time immemorial. Despite the veil of secrecy that hangs about their private lives, leopards are well studied and have been the stars of many wildlife films. They are typically solitary, males and females coming together only briefly to mate. The male's presence is manifest, however, as he continues to defend his territory, which may include the ranges of several females. He takes no part in the raising of his cubs, which will stay with their mother for just under the first two years of their lives. Although sometimes aggressively driven away by their mothers, young leopards may still remain within their natal ranges for some time while learning how to become expert hunters. During this 'probation' the mother may still make food available to her offspring.

Life for newly independent young leopards is far from easy, particularly the task of finding and successfully defending territories of their own. Inexperience and their smaller stature usually preclude all-out territorial battles with established adults. And so the youngsters, especially the females, often have to settle for territories peripheral to well-treed drainage lines, dongas and other areas of thick bush which are usually held by the most powerful and successful adults. This means that young leopards are frequently forced into occupying more open areas, where prey is less plentiful and the lack of cover makes hunting even more difficult. On the brighter side, however, there is far less competition for prey from established adults, and the more resourceful youngsters will not only survive, but will grow in size and prowess until, at some opportune moment, they are in a position to challenge for a better place in the neighbourhood.

1, 2, 3

**1** *The wild hibiscus produces butter-yellow flowers in summer.*
**2** *A dotted blue butterfly displays its boldly patterned underwing.*
**3** *A chinspot batis sitting on its lichen-camouflaged nest. This tiny bird is widespread and often seen foraging in the tree canopy, usually in pairs, or sometimes as a member of a mixed feeding party. The song of the male is a rather plaintive fluting, but when alarmed it rasps out a harsh* ch-ch-ch-ch, *rather like the sound of sandpaper being rubbed on wood.*
**4** *The flowers of* Crinum buphanoides *are unusual in that they face directly upwards.*

4

# Hot and Humid

SUMMER IN THE LOWVELD can be stiflingly hot and, if the rains have been good, oppressively humid. It is a time of great bounty, with rivers in full flow and food for all. It is also a time of lush green grass, trees in full leaf and flowers in bloom. It is easy to overlook the many flowering shrubs, climbers and herbs of the Lowveld, dwarfed as they are by towering trees and often hidden from immediate view deep in some shady grove or rocky crevice – but they are there.

Some, however, are not shy and flaunt their beauty for all to see. Queen amongst them has to be the gloriosa or flame lily, which is widely found throughout the Lowveld. Using its slender tendrils to cling to its host for support, it clambers over shrubs and the boles of trees, then colours the landscape with a fiery display of blooms through vibrant reds and oranges to deep buttercup yellows, the long, twisted petals leaping from their calyxes like small tongues of flame.

Grass, shrubs and trees, here and there dotted with the colour of their flowers, merge to form an almost impenetrable curtain of green. It can be a frustrating time for game-viewing, as the animals easily conceal themselves amongst the dense foliage. Even those a mere few metres away can move by unnoticed. They are also well dispersed, taking good advantage of the many watering spots that are now scattered through the landscape.

But some animals cannot pass unseen, for this is the time of year when that most prolific of all the Lowveld's antelope, the impala, commands centre stage. Except, possibly, during the autumn rutting season, for most of the year its lithe, glossy-brown form is largely dismissed as a standard element in the Lowveld landscape. Come early summer, though, with the promise of plentiful food to sustain the females' milk supply, impala lambs are born in their thousands. Within a few days of their birth, and already steady on their long, spindly legs, the lambs are introduced back into the herd, where they associate in crèches with other new-borns, only seeking out their mothers to suckle or for protection.

**Above:** *A languid bushveld scene in the fullness of summer – the crowns of the trees lining the river are deep green, and the waterway itself is edged by thick stands of reeds.*
**5** *The crimson, balled flowerhead of* Scadoxus multiflorus.
**6** *The strikingly beautiful flame lily occurs widely throughout the northern regions of the Lowveld.*
**7** *A mopane pomegranate in full flower. A species found in hot, low-lying parts of the Lowveld, this shrub or small tree bears clusters of bright yellow flowers soon after the first summer rains.*

5

6 7

1 2

# Lords of the Air

FOR ANYONE WITH MORE than a passing interest in birds, the early months of summer are a very special time. Like the trees and wild flowers coming into leaf and bloom, the birds, too, promise hot, moist months of plenitude. Everywhere their industry is in evidence, as the males of many species break out into their often-brilliant summer uniforms, engage in elaborate courtship displays, and start nest-building with a purpose that suggests that tomorrow simply will not do.

The majority of the birds that occur in the Lowveld are resident throughout the year. But many are there as visitors from other parts of Africa or from further afield, having flown thousands of kilometres from the steppes of Eurasia and elsewhere in the northern hemisphere. Some, like the pygmy and grey-hooded kingfishers and the lesser striped swallow, come to breed whereas others, including the white stork that is often seen striding through open bush, arrive only to exploit the bountiful food available. But it's not just the sight of these migrants that excites the senses, for their calls also signal their welcome return – the harsh trill of the woodland kingfisher, for example, and the somewhat plaintive fluting of the Diederik cuckoo.

The Lowveld, too, is home, either permanently or as a summer refuge, to those lords of the air – the eagles, hawks, kites, falcons and harriers – that occupy the top end of the food chain. Resident species include the bateleur, common throughout the region and easily identified by its characteristic 'rocking' motion as it rides the thermals, ever watchful for a potential meal.

Largest of all the raptors of the bush is the martial eagle, with its striking white front spotted with brown. Sightings of this massive bird are always on the cards, as it prefers open bush and high, exposed perches from which it hunts the squirrels, monitors and birds that make up most of its diet. But for sheer beauty, none of the other birds of prey can match the fish eagle. With the immaculate white of its head and breast contrasting with the rich auburn of its wings and lower body plumage, it is truly an icon of the African bush. Nowhere close to water would the landscape be complete without this handsome eagle, and the bush would seem empty without its mournful, drawn-out cry floating across the thick Lowveld air.

**Above:** *White-backed vultures, the common vulture of the Lowveld, mill around the carcass of a zebra. Once the large birds have settled in to feed they dominate the site, allowing no other vulture species a look-in.*
**1** *The magnificent, powerfully built martial eagle takes prey as large as the common duiker.*
**2** *The European roller is a fairly common visitor, migrating to southern Africa and India from its summer breeding grounds in Europe, the Middle East and western Asia.*

**3** *A white stork displays the impressive wingspan that has borne it thousands of kilometres from the Palaearctic regions.*
**4** *European swallows congregate in March and April prior to departing for their northern breeding grounds.*

3

4

53

# Golden Light

BY MID-APRIL the debilitating heat of summer has begun to fade. Daytime temperatures can still be high, but the evenings are becoming cooler, sometimes with just a hint of the chilly nights that lie ahead. It is a wonderful, mellow time of golden light and rich, warm landscapes as the leaves of deciduous trees begin to turn colour and fall.

Gone are the vibrant shades of summer-flowering trees and shrubs, but here and there along the river margins the haphazard tangle of a red spike-thorn tree shows off clusters of sweetly scented blooms. From a short distance away these delicate, star-shaped white flowers can look almost like a light dusting of snow on the evergreen leaves. Later, the reddish, berry-like fruits will provide a welcome larder for birds, and the leaves will feed elephants, black rhino, giraffes and browsing antelope. Traditional healers, too, are familiar with the red spike-thorn, using extracts of the roots and thorns to treat coughs and colds.

Of all the creatures of the bush, it is perhaps the birds that sense most acutely the coming cold. European swallows, easily identified by their habit of skimming above roads and often settling on the tarmac – sometimes in large numbers – are beginning to congregate in anticipation of the long haul back to their summer breeding grounds in Europe. This may be the last chance to see many of the cuckoos that visit southern Africa to escape the harsh winters of the northern hemisphere. Soon heading northward, too, will be the European and broad-billed rollers and the bold woodland kingfisher, whose strident alarm-clock trill is so much part of the Lowveld summer.

**Far left:** *In the soft evening light of autumn, the turning foliage of marula trees seems to glow with a richness of flowers rather than leaves. Soon the leaves will fall, leaving the trees bereft of colour until the red flowers begin to appear in early August.*
**1** *An African wild cat on the hunt. These small felines are widespread, hunting mainly in the evening and early morning.*
**2** *A toad grasshopper of the family Pamphagidae.*
**3** *Autumn leaves and the distinctive fruit pods of the large-fruited bushwillow.*

1

2

# A Cold, Dry Time

THE LOWVELD IS NOW in the grip of a cold and dry season. There is a stillness, too, as night-time temperatures plummet and there seems to be a great reluctance among the creatures of the veld to be out and about. The orchestral chaos of insects and frogs giving full expression to their summer repertoire has ceased, and only sporadically does the mournful cry of a jackal or the graveyard cackle of a hyaena lift the cloak of silence. Campfires take on a significance beyond just cooking and conviviality, and are now to be huddled around while sipping hot coffee, or something stronger.

But like all seasons, winter in the bush has its pleasures too. Crisp, clear nights are a time to look upward into the heavens, where a whole new wonderland is revealed by a steady hand and a reasonable pair of binoculars. Can it really be possible that there are so many heavenly bodies? Such is the confusion of stars that it can be difficult to pick out even those stalwarts of the southern skies, the Southern Cross, Orion's Belt and the bold outline of the Scorpion. And the Milky Way and Clouds of Magellan are like diamonds cast in infinite numbers on a swathe of black velvet.

Winter is also a good time for game-viewing – the best, according to many – as the thick mantle of summer green has long since died back, making it possible to see for some distance through the tangle of branches and undergrowth. Water, too, is in short supply – the ephemeral pans and streams have dried once more to an uninviting dustiness, their positions marked in the drab landscape only by the resilience of a few evergreen trees and shrubs. The animals, predator and prey alike, dare not stray too far from any permanent supply, and along the routes that follow watercourses or lead to waterholes the chances of witnessing a kill may be higher than during times of greater lushness.

Left: *A herd of buffalo on the move. The earth is bone-dry underfoot and the heavy impact of hundreds of hooves sends a cloud of dust billowing up, all but obscuring the weak winter sun.*

**1** *A bull elephant uses his trunk to shower himself with dry sand.*

**2** *Blue wildebeest and zebra mill about in the sparse, dry veld surrounding a waterhole, while helmeted guineafowl scratch away in the never-ending search for seeds.*

1

2

# Life in a Dustbowl

A BITING WIND swirls around the veld, sweeping the desiccated sand and bits of dried vegetation into messy brown clouds. Everywhere there is dust. The bare branches of roadside trees and bushes, the cars of tourists passing through, the animals – all are wearing dun-coloured coats.

The earth around a water trough – a legacy of a conservation management policy whose aim it was to compensate for interrupted migration routes – is trampled into barren dryness. Nothing grows within a perimeter that widens day by day, relentlessly pushing back the fringe of brittle sticks that a few months earlier were thick with leaves.

A skeletal windmill turns slowly and draws a pulse of life-giving water from deep below the Lowveld floor. A lone elephant bull siphons the liquid seemingly faster than the pump can replace it. Some distance off, a dust cloud billows above the bare woodland canopy and advances slowly towards the waterhole. As it draws closer it becomes apparent that the cloud is driven not by the wind but by the hooves of a mixed herd of wildebeest and zebra making the daily pilgrimage to slake their thirst. For a moment they mill about, wary and unsure. Then the elephant gives way and the first few among the new arrivals make their way tentatively towards the trough.

1

# Drawn to Water

AS WINTER DRAWS IN, the watercourses of the Lowveld, including those that have flowed strongly thanks to good summer rains, begin to slow and dry up. Even the large perennial rivers lose their powerful flow and are reduced to a series of pools threaded together by thin ribbons of water. At best, backwaters, vleis and oxbow lakes are little more than thick, muddy soups; most, however, are dry, the cracked mud looking like ill-fitting pieces of a jigsaw puzzle.

Now the animals must rely on the few remaining waterholes to see them through the long dry months of winter. It is a stressful time for many herbivores, for as the available grazing and foliage surrounding the waterholes is inexorably consumed, so they have to expend more and more energy in moving between the water and their feeding grounds. It is a bonus time for game-viewing at waterholes, though, and a bonus time for lions, leopards and cheetah, for now they need only to stay within striking distance of the waterholes to pick off a meal as the herds come down to drink.

But this is very simplistic. In reality, the ecology of waterholes is highly complex. Some species such as waterbuck and impala have evolved in relatively well-watered areas and tend not to move far from available supplies. Others, including roan, buffalo, zebra, wildebeest, tsessebe and elephant, have adapted to a less reliable water resource and can survive while roaming considerable distances in search of liquid. At the far end of the scale are species such as eland and small browsing antelope – grey duiker and steenbok, for instance – that are largely independent of water and can survive for long periods without drinking as long as there is sufficient moisture in their browse.

When waterholes become completely dry, then game relies on the digging abilities of certain of the Lowveld animals. Baboons, rhinos and zebras are able to excavate for water but, without question, elephants are the best diggers. In the sandy patches that mark the outer curves of river bends they dig their 'wells' down to considerable depths.

2    3

# A Welcome Warmth

THE LONG HAUL OF WINTER is all but over. The days are beginning to lengthen and a welcome warmth bathes the land. All that is needed now is for the life-giving rains to fall.

First to give a show of faith that a time of plenty is near are the trees. From as early as August the sjambok pods have provided colourful relief in a sea of brown, and their massed yellow blossoms still crown the parent trees well ahead of the foliage to follow. The sausage trees have also long graced the drab Lowveld landscape with their rose-red, cup-like flowers, and the apple-leaf trees, too, come into bloom, their generous bunches of fragrant flowers showing dramatically against new foliage. The petals fall easily to carpet the ground in soft purple, while also adding a splash of colour are the deep purple, pea-like flowers of tree wistarias. Attractive sprays of crimson sprout from the briefly leafless weeping boer-beans, the last few big, open seed pods still hanging tenaciously from bare branches.

Then, in November, particularly along the Kruger Park's watercourses near Malelane in the south, Pretoriuskop, and Punda Maria in the far north, the vigorous climber Pride-of-de-Kaap erupts into a profusion of large, brick-red sprays.

But perhaps the greatest miracle of all is that of the massive baobabs, which offer their delicate, perfumed blooms for little longer than a single night to the fruit bats charged with the responsibility of carrying pollen from one tree to the next.

**1** *The brick-red, bell-shaped flowers of Pride-of-De-Kaap make their appearance in early November and continue throughout the height of summer into February. This scrambling shrub usually occurs in rocky areas or near streams. It is an important food source for two butterfly species of the* Virachola *genus.*

**Above:** *Knobthorn trees in full blossom. Creamy flower spikes covering the leafless trees in August and September are one of the first signs that the worst of winter is past and that the warmth of early summer is on its way.*

**2** *Male kudu lie up beneath a sjambok pod. Like the blossoms of the knobthorn, the flowers of the sjambok pod first appear in August while the tree is still leafless.*

**3** *Giraffe take advantage of the shade of an apple-leaf tree laden with fragrant, purple flowers.*

2   3

**Left:** *Helmeted guineafowl scuttle about in the fading light of late afternoon. Guineafowl are highly gregarious, especially out of the breeding season when flocks of several hundred birds may be seen.*
**1** *As the day draws to a close, warthogs head for the safety of their burrows, often the disused retreats of aardvarks. Warthog piglets are born in the burrows and grow rapidly; within three weeks they can be seen grazing, but they do not stray too far from their refuge.*
**2** *Unlike the diurnal warthog, the spotted hyaena rests up for the major part of the day. It rises in the late afternoon and quickly moves off to hunt and scavenge.*

# Lengthening Shadows

THE LONG LOWVELD SIESTA draws to a close and signs of activity can be perceived once more. Somewhere a cheetah is hunting, trying hard to down an impala and then to eat its fill before, as is often the case, it is robbed by more powerful competitors, especially spotted hyaenas and lions. Elsewhere a pack of wild dogs lazily come to their feet to begin the long, elaborate exchange of greetings among members of the group, a ritual accompanied by much high-pitched whining and chattering.

A warm amber glow clothes the Lowveld as shadows lengthen. Barely making a sound, a column of elephants, a breeding herd of females and their offspring, tread purposefully down a well-worn path towards the river. The older ones keep together, but the exuberant youngsters can hardly contain themselves, agitating and jostling towards the front of the line. They are clearly eager to reach the cooling water and, once on the narrow floodplain, they break rank and move rapidly towards the river, their trunks reaching forward in anticipation.

The rude antics of the young elephants startle a skittish herd of wildebeest already at the water's edge and the ungainly antelope display a deceptive turn of speed as they explode into action. Nesting blacksmith plovers are also disturbed by the ruckus and vent their spleen in characteristic fashion by angrily haranguing and dive-bombing the newcomers. A bold display, but essentially futile, for the elephants pay no attention at all as they take occupation of the shallows.

1

2

**Far right:** *A flock of white pelicans sets off towards its overnight roost.*
**1** *A handsome kudu bull stands in perfect relief against the setting sun. The coming darkness heralds a time of great stress for the daytime grazers and browsers of the Lowveld, as now the large carnivores, well adapted to hunting in poor light conditions, are about.*
**2** *The zebra is also a daytime animal; these two are beginning to move from their pasture to their open night-time resting areas.*

# Early Evening

THERE IS NO LINGERING DUSK in the Lowveld and night comes quickly. The great orange orb of the sun drops hurriedly towards the horizon, and then, as it touches the distant escarpment, it seems to balance there for no more than a moment or two before continuing its timeless journey.

For a few short minutes the western sky is lava-red moving through an arc of softer, pastel shades of pink, yellow and blue to deep indigo towards the far side of the world. The colours of the landscape quickly fill in until all is thrown into a uniform inky relief. The herd of elephants down at the river have drunk their fill and are now moving off into the gathering darkness, while overhead a flight of raucous hadeda ibises wing towards their roost.

For a moment an eerie silence cloaks the Lowveld, as if its inhabitants are adjusting to the sudden change of day into night. Then, a loud grunting reverberates up the valley – hippos in a prelude to their wading ashore for a night of grazing – and some way off a black-backed jackal moans into the dark. Another Lowveld night is under way.

1  2

**Left:** *Lions slake their thirst at a waterhole. These cats will drink regularly where water is available, and particularly after feeding on a kill.*

# Night Drive

SLOWLY THE YELLOW-WHITE BEAM pierces the darkness, washing the base of the nearby tree line in ghostly light. Back and forth, back and forth it moves, expertly guided by the tracker sitting in the jump seat on the Land Rover bonnet.

A practised flick of the light cautions the ranger behind the wheel to halt. The beam steadies on a small clearing in the grass and the tracker points down the shaft of light. Two red pinpricks glow like tiny embers and then bounce off into taller grass as if attached to springs. 'Springhaas,' the tracker whispers, using the Afrikaans name for the springhare. Not actually a member of the rabbit and hare family at all, the springhare is a nocturnal rodent with long, powerful hindlegs that enable it to bound expertly, for all the world like some small kangaroo that has mysteriously found its way onto the African continent.

It is the first sighting of the evening, and the attention of the eight guests occupying the vehicle is riveted, each one of them straining for a sighting of this strange creature. Springhares often move about in groups, so it is not long before the tracker picks out another and this one stays long enough for everyone to get a good look.

Other creatures are caught in the blinding beam of the million-candle-power light, but the tracker is careful not to hold them in its mesmerising glare and shines it as obliquely as possible. Nightjars, fruit bats, owls and even a rarely seen striped weasel, scurrying arch-back across the track, are all part of the parade.

But the real purpose of the night drive is for the tracker and ranger to find lion, leopard and hyaena. As fascinating as the smaller creatures of the night may be, the guests are all hoping to see the big predators. And they are not to be disappointed. Another vehicle calls in to report a leopard kill and, after a brief exchange over the short-wave radio, the ranger steers off down a track to the left and then, a short, bone-jolting ride later, he slows to veer off into the bush. Now there is no track and the ranger carefully picks his way through the bush, cautioning his guests to watch out for raking acacia thorns. Up ahead lights flicker – the other party – and the next moment the vehicle pulls into a clearing, at the centre of which a female leopard and two youngsters are feasting off a freshly downed impala. It is the climax of a night-time game drive in the African bush, and an experience that will live forever in the minds of those who witness it.

**1** *A game tracker expertly wields a powerful spotlight, picking out nocturnal animals for the benefit of lodge guests as their vehicle moves slowly through the bush. Little escapes the probing beam, from a hippo grazing in open grassland to a tiny chameleon on the branch of a tree.*
**2** *The eyes of impala, reflecting the oblique glare of headlights, betray the animals' presence.*
**3** *Barred owls huddle together. Like a number of other owls, this species takes prey by dropping onto it from a perch.*
**4** *Lion cubs at play.*

3

4

1  2

# Heard, but Seldom Seen

WHEN DARKNESS FALLS in the Lowveld, even the most seasoned game ranger, if he's honest, will admit to an edginess and an added sense of caution. Even in broad daylight the bush holds real dangers for the unwary, but at night it can become downright menacing. The most powerful of torches can light up only a fraction of the surroundings, and beyond their narrow beams the dark is even more impenetrable to the human eye. The hours of darkness belong without question to those creatures whose senses of smell, hearing and sight are honed well beyond the human range.

A game drive at night under the expert direction of a ranger and his tracker will reveal some of the lesser nocturnal Lowveld inhabitants, but even a lifetime in the wilds of Africa will result only in the occasional encounter with some animals. For the most part the night passes in a series of unidentifiable rustles and snuffling sounds, with now and then the high-pitched squeal of some small creature as it meets its fate.

In addition to the well-known bigger cats and hyaenas, the Lowveld hosts many other carnivores, many of which are almost exclusively nocturnal. The agile small-spotted and large-spotted genets for example, and the civet which is often taken for one of the cat family but in fact, like the genets, is a member of the Viverridae, a large and heterogeneous family that includes mongooses and the suricate. Honey badgers are also about at night – rough, tough and fearless enough to give a good account of themselves even against a lion if cornered. Their main concern, however, is not to brawl with all comers, but to find food which ranges from spiders and scorpions to birds, reptiles, bee larvae and honey.

Almost exclusively arboreal, and often giving their presence away with blood-curdling, child-like cries, are the bushbabies. The spine-chilling calls of these nocturnal primates belie an otherwise inoffensive existence spent grubbing around in the woodland canopy for insects and eating the gum of trees. Among the larger, but also harmless creatures of the night are porcupines, a favourite but troublesome food of lions, and the very seldom seen aardvark, whose prodigious digging prowess is put to good effect in tearing down termite mounds to reach the insects that are its sole diet.

1  *The serval is easily identified by its long neck and legs, and its huge ears.*
2  *The African civet is normally silent but has a deep growl and an explosive cough, both of which are used to good effect if an individual feels threatened or cornered.*

**Right:** *A greater bushbaby, or galago, in its typically arboreal habitat. Nocturnal, long-tailed woolly primates, bushbabies have a distinctively African lineage more than 20 million years old. They are shy and secretive, but their plaintive yowls cut eerily through the darkness – a characteristic sound of the bushveld night.*

**3** *The spotted dikkop makes its loud, piping call mostly at night, and especially after rain.*

**4** *The European nightjar is a fairly common summer visitor. Although mostly silent, in flight it occasionally calls* coo-ic, *and* quick-quick-quick *when perching.*

# Around the Campfire

AFTER A LONG DAY in the bush there is nothing quite as relaxing as a leisurely barbecue and then settling down around the friendly glow of a fire. Every now and then someone rises to throw a fresh log onto the glowing embers, in the process setting off a fleeting display of orange-red sparks. There is a sense of comradeship, and one feels safe and at peace with the world. Against the shrill chorus of insects and frogs, the far-off rumble of a lion and the odd whoop of a hyaena, the conversation flows, moving easily from highlights of the day's game-viewing to moments of deep reflection on the profound effect the bush has on the human psyche, and then to humour, legends and personal recollections – suitably embellished, of course.

The convivial atmosphere around a campfire can also prove irresistible to the prankster. In his book *South African Eden*, James Stevenson-Hamilton tells of the time when South African Railways ran a popular tour of the Lowveld that included, at the good colonel's behest, a stopover in the Sabie Game Reserve, the fore-

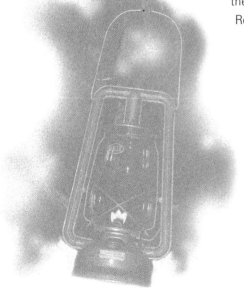

runner of the Kruger National Park. Highlights of the trip included short walks in the bush and sitting around a blazing camp fire in the evening 'alternately singing choruses and shivering with delight at the idea of being watched, from the dark bush close at hand, by the hungry eyes of beasts of prey...'.

A steward on the train managed to procure a lion skin and on occasion would draw it around himself and 'come crawling stealthily into the ring of firelight, to be greeted with shrieks from the more timid of the ladies, while the bolder of the men would assume protective attitudes'. As if this were not enough, the police sergeant stationed at Sabi Bridge could produce a very life-like imitation of a lion's roar by blowing through a long glass tube and 'as his confederate was advancing, would, from a place of concealment, provide the necessary vocal accompaniment'.

Stevenson-Hamilton was deeply encouraged by the interest of the passengers in the wildlife of the Lowveld and this added to his conviction that if the national park scheme were allowed to mature, it would become highly popular and an asset to the country. How right he was.

1

**Above:** *Sitting around a warm, friendly blaze, sharing companionship and experiences, is one of the deep pleasures of being in the African bush. In the early part of the evening, however, especially in the summer months, the croaks and calls of frogs and a myriad insects can all but drown out human conversation. Later, quiet settles over the camp, broken only by the intermittent cries of animals and the spit and crackle of burning logs.*
**1** *Kettles boil over a cooking fire.*
**2** *A white-faced owl perches among the thorns of an acacia tree.*
**3** *Spotted hyaenas skulk around at the edge of the light cast by a campfire.*

2    3

**Right:** *Having brought down a zebra, lions immediately set about devouring the carcass. Although larger prey animals are preferred when they are plentiful, lions are remarkably adaptable in their diet. In times of scarcity, rats, reptiles, fish and even groundnuts are eaten.*

**1** *Vultures mass in a tree above a kill at dusk. They usually roost in trees, and in the morning thermals will carry them high above the landscape. Soon a carcass will be spotted and then, in a rapidly descending spiral, the great birds will home in to feed.*

1

# *Killing Fields*

THE SENSE OF TRANQUILLITY that one feels around a campfire is, of course, illusory. For 'out there', beyond the comforting circle of light thrown by the burning logs, the timeless drama of predator and prey is remorselessly played out. And it is not only the drama between hunter and hunted, but often that between hunter and hunter as well.

The leopard, for example, seems to have everything it could want: power, agility, excellent night vision, great stealth... But it is solitary and therein lies its weakness, for the lion and the spotted hyaena are social animals that rely on co-operation and numbers for their success.

Although not as vulnerable as the cheetah after making a kill, the leopard generally does not have long to feed before the attention of its rivals is attracted by the noise of the scuffle or the smell of freshly spilt blood. For this reason the leopard has a well-developed tactic of using its great strength to carry the carcass of its victim high into the protective branches of a large tree, there to consume its meal in relative peace.

Caching the prey in a tree may work well against hyaenas, but lions can climb, and surprisingly well for animals of their bulk. If hungry enough, they will lose no time in scrambling up after the leopard in an attempt to wrestle the carcass to the ground. Although the leopard will often make a great show of protecting its property, it eventually has to give way in an unequal battle.

Likewise, if cornered on the ground with its prey, it is bound to lose against both lions and hyaenas. One-on-one, the leopard is probably more than a match for the larger and more heavily built hyaena, but it simply cannot risk injury by entering into all-out combat. And so, while one or more of a pack of hyaenas worry at the leopard, the others move in and often simply steal the carcass.

Few of these countless night-time life-and-death dramas are witnessed by visitors to the Lowveld, but as the air warms in the morning that follows, swirling assemblies of vultures and other raptors mark the sites of kills.

**2** *A leopard caches its kill in a tree, where it can feed without the unwelcome attentions of competitors.*
**3** *Reputed to be lazy scavengers always ready to take over a kill, spotted hyaenas are, in fact, also consummate hunters in their own right.*
**4** *Male lions, too, have a reputation for indolence and for commandeering kills made by the pride females, but if the occasion demands, they are highly competent in pulling down game.*

2

3 4

# Ever the Opportunists

BY NO STRETCH of the imagination is the hyaena the most beautiful animal of the African savanna; it looks out of proportion, with its massive, almost bear-like head and its shoulders sloping down to small hindquarters. It lacks the power and regal bearing of the lion and has none of the grace of the leopard or cheetah.

And, as if its disadvantage in looks is not enough, the hyaena is also maligned as a lowly, craven scavenger, an image not improved by the other-worldly howls and cackles that mark its presence in the Lowveld night. But, as with many things in life and in the bush in particular, things are not always as they seem. In reality, the hyaena is not the miscreant it is made out to be but, in fact, a wily predator and generally as successful a hunter as any member of the cat family.

Hyaenas are relative newcomers to the African stage. These robust carnivores may look more like dogs than anything else, but genetic studies reveal evolutionary links to mongooses and civets. They possibly originated in Asia only about ten million years ago, while ancestors of the striped and spotted hyaenas, probably looking very similar to the living species of today, evolved as recently as five million years ago.

The secret of the hyaena's success lies in its versatility as a hunter and a scavenger. Ever the opportunist, it will worry cheetahs and leopards off their kills, but if driven by hunger a single individual is capable of running down and killing a fully grown wildebeest several times its own body weight.

Although the hyaena's movements may seem awkward and ungainly, it covers the ground surprisingly fast and can lope along tirelessly, maintaining a speed of about ten kilometres an hour. When the occasion demands, however, it easily changes up a gear or two and can gallop at an impressive 50 kilometres an hour for some distance.

The golden rule of the hyaena, though, is the path of least resistance and active hunting is a last resort. More often, a pack of hyaenas will lurk on the outskirts of a herd, patiently waiting for the right moment to make their move on the sick, young and disabled. Unlike rival predators which are not equipped to devour the entire carcass, hyaenas eat everything but the rumen. Bones, horns, hooves and even teeth are shattered by their own powerful teeth that are set in massive jaws, and all is completely digested within 24 hours.

1

2

**Right:** *A clan of spotted hyaenas at a kill, with a black-backed jackal in attendance. The impressive bulk of the hyaenas is clearly evident – a large female (females are somewhat bigger than males) can outweigh a male leopard.*
**1** *A female spotted hyaena with her offspring.*
**2** *A young hyaena. The juveniles are ready to take their place at a kill by the age of eight months, but will continue to suckle until they are about 18 months old.*

# Sociable Cats

EVEN WHEN SLEEPING or just lolling under a tree during the heat of the day, lions exude power. Maybe it's just the flick of a tail or a half-hearted swipe at an errant cub, but it is enough to suggest the great physical strength of these big, blond predators. The pervasive 'off-duty' attitude is also deceptive, for the slightest irregular sound – the whirring of a camera motor drive, perhaps – is enough to make heads lift instantly and several pairs of tawny eyes fix themselves towards the intrusion.

Of all the cats, the lion is the only species to live permanently in association with others of its kind. Cheetahs are something of an exception, but even in their case, groupings are seldom more than a mother with her grown cubs, or adult siblings that have remained together. Cheetah liaisons certainly lack the durability and complexity of lion society.

Superficially, there are similarities between lion prides and families of elephants, for just as the matriarch is the focus of the tight bonds that exist in elephant herds, so the lioness, often together with her sisters and/or cousins, is at the centre of pride cohesion. Female cubs born to the pride lionesses usually bond with the pride for life, but when male cubs reach puberty they are generally ousted by their mothers.

Male lions are not a prerequisite of pride structure, and there are a number of well-documented examples of thriving all-female prides. More often than not, though, a coalition of two or more adult males forms part of the pride. But their presence is transitory, for they have claimed their positions by right of conquest. Within a few years it is almost certain that they in turn will be overthrown in a fierce and noisy battle – but usually one that is not life-threatening – by a pair of younger, stronger males. And even if such a *coup d'état* did not occur, it is likely that the males would anyway move on.

That lions co-operate in hunting for food has long been understood as fundamental in their evolution as sociable cats, and stories abound that tell of lions as supreme strategists co-ordinating their efforts to outwit prey. Few of these claims stand up to close scrutiny, however; the reality is that a hunt is more likely a fairly loosely organised affair in which individuals act independently. As lions on the hunt move through the bush, each is ready to take advantage of any opportunity that presents itself. Thus hunting is often a matter of coming across prey rather than the elaborate playing out of any predetermined group effort. Nevertheless, teamwork does undoubtedly exist, particularly when the combined strength of several lions is required to bring down and subdue large and dangerous prey such as buffalo.

**Below:** *Lionesses and their young at rest. Lionesses, often sisters and/or female cousins, are the focus of pride activity, and they have usually remained in the same pride from birth.*
**1** *A lioness feeds her youngsters.*
**2** *As inquisitive as any other young animal, a lion cub exploring its surroundings balances precariously in a tree.*

**3** *There is a great deal of physical contact between the members of a pride. Reunions, particularly, are characterised by head rubbing and licking.*
**4** *Two cubs playing.*

1 2

# In Praise of Trees

IT IS NOT SURPRISING that trees evoke in us such a strong emotional response – especially those huge specimens that soar to the heights of multi-storey buildings. They seem so powerful, permanent and reliable. Stories of magic trees and haunted forests crowd the myths and legends of almost every culture on earth. Their association with man through the ages has been more than close, it has been inseparable. We have, and still do, use trees for food, shelter, fuel, clothing, transport, weapons, medicine … the list goes on.

Well over 200 species of trees occur in the Lowveld, and if you add to these the 180-odd species of woody plants that do not generally grow to tree size in the region but do so elsewhere and are therefore regarded as trees, the number grows to about 400 – almost 50 per cent of the total tree flora of Africa south of the Zambezi and Kunene rivers.

Trees are the very fabric of the Lowveld landscape, abundant and massive in areas where perennial rivers and high rainfall support such growth. Elsewhere, though, they may be few and far between, or low and scrubby where soil condition and the availability of water are less conducive to their thriving.

Wherever they grow, trees exist in close association with the browsers and fruit-eaters that depend on them for food, and the many other animals that find safety and shelter in their great spreading canopies. Some, like the baobab, are virtual ecosystems in their own right.

Trees are the very lifeblood of the Lowveld, for without them the remaining wilderness of the region would not exist as we know it. The great diversity of wildlife that makes the game reserves of the Lowveld one of the natural treasures of the world would simply not be there.

3

1 | 2

*1 The graceful spread of a jackal-berry tree, so named for the great love jackals are believed to have for the fallen fruits. The juicy berries are also a firm favourite with monkeys.*
*2 The umbrella thorn is one of the quintessential trees of the African savanna.*

4

**Right:** *A dense stand of sycamore figs in a riverine forest. The fruits are rich and juicy, and bearing trees attract a variety of animals, from feeding parties of birds, monkeys and baboons to warthogs, antelope and even rhino.*
**3** *Burchell's starlings usually occur in pairs and small parties in savanna woodland. They nest in natural holes in trees.*
**4** *Like many birds, the arrow-marked babbler finds its food – both insects and fruits – in a tree's canopy.*

1

**Left:** *An elephant rocks a marula tree, bringing down a shower of the sweet yellow fruits that are rich in vitamin C and much favoured by the great beasts. It is popularly thought that elephants become intoxicated from eating fermenting marula fruits, but this notion is the stuff of myth rather than fact.*

**1** *Dense clusters of the plumlike fruits of the sycamore fig. The fruits are borne throughout the year and are much sought after by many mammals and birds.*

4

2    3

# *Lives Intertwined*

**2** *Mushrooms growing in elephant dung.*
**3** *A red-billed oxpecker gleans ectoparasites on a buffalo.*
**4** *A weeping boer-bean tree has taken root in a termite mound, sustained by the water in its cavities.*

NOTHING IN THE WILD happens in isolation, and the Lowveld is no exception. In addition to obvious links in the food chain – from microbes and insects devouring fallen and living vegetation through the gamut of larger insectivorous and plant-eating animals right up to the carnivores – there is a multitude of other, subtle associations that play vital roles in the life cycles of many life forms. And each in its way underlies the miracle of evolution.

For instance, there is the ancient alliance between wild figs and a group of wasps. The flowers of the fig tree are unusual in that their stamens and stigmas are not exposed to facilitate pollination. Instead, they bloom hidden and enclosed within a fleshy inflorescence known as the syconium. The female wasp is attracted to the 'fruit' and enters it through a tiny opening, losing her wings in the process. Inside her tomb, she pollinates the flowers, lays her eggs and dies. From the eggs, the male wasps hatch first and impregnate the still-developing females. Then the females hatch, deliberately gather pollen and leave via tunnels that the males excavate before they die. Once in the open, the females fly off in search of a new wild fig to service, so enacting another cycle in a partnership that has existed for at least 60 million years and that if interrupted would result in the extinction of both wasp and tree.

Almost in the same league, but somewhat more one-sided, is the story of a small moth that would certainly die out if elephants were to disappear from the savanna landscape. Somewhat ironically, however, the moth's survival can only be ensured by the death of an individual elephant. The female moth lays her eggs in the soles of a dead elephant which, being the hardest part of the animal's skin, are the last to decay. Thus they provide a safe, protein-rich refuge for the developing larvae. Other organisms dependent on elephants are dung beetle species that rely almost solely on elephant droppings as nests for their eggs and developing larvae, and certain tree species whose seeds must pass through the gut of an elephant to ensure successful germination.

The elephant's role in the wild is, of course, huge. Because of its size and great need for food and water, it has the ability like no other species except man to adapt and alter its environment. Even its seemingly destructive habit of pushing over trees has results that are beneficial for other species. The foliage and pods of tall knobthorn trees, for example, are favourites amongst many browsers, but it is usually only the giraffe that can reach high enough to feed on them. By pushing the trees over to reach the leaves for themselves, elephants also make the succulent upper foliage available to a wide range of smaller browsers.

1  2

# Africa's Giants

IT IS HARD TO THINK of another animal that has been as observed, studied, hunted and photographed to the extent that the African elephant has. More than any other land mammal, with the possible exception of the great apes, the elephant evokes a deep response in the human mind. Its size alone makes it an awesome beast and worthy of respect. But it is so much more than just a great beast with a commanding physical presence; the elephant is the embodiment of wisdom and is imbued with a complex sense of social behaviour that includes caring for its fellows, especially the young of a herd.

Elephants had their beginnings in Africa and have an ancient lineage that stretches back in time to a mere five million years after the last dinosaurs became extinct. And since the first hominids walked erect across the wide expanses of the African landscape, elephants and man have lived alongside one another. For most of this time their co-existence has been peaceable enough, but since the late nineteenth century the two have been increasingly set against each other. Wanton hunting and poaching for the elephant's valuable ivory has taken many populations to the brink of extinction, and sometimes beyond. Furthermore,

the increase in the human population has placed a huge burden on the land, and competition for *Lebensraum* has thrown man and beast into further conflict.

Today it is really only in major wildlife reserves that the elephant enjoys a modicum of security. But elephants are successful breeders, and in fenced reserves or conservation areas surrounded by human development, problems soon occur. Habitat is devastated to satisfy voracious appetites, and conflict arises with neighbouring communities whose crops are threatened by marauding elephants. And so, the management of elephant populations is one of the most hotly debated conservation issues of our time.

The overriding dilemma, though, has to be faced squarely: in the face of man's needs and demands on the landscape the elephant will lose out. It is a strange feeling indeed to see elephants as they should be, roaming freely across the savanna in their closely knit maternal herds, and to reflect that we are witnessing the twilight years of a species much older than our own. If the elephant were only a dreaded adversary of man, then its demise would hardly raise a whimper. But this is not so, and in its passing we know that we are losing a part of ourselves.

**Right:** *A baby elephant seldom strays far from its mother, who is highly sensitive to its every need.*
**1** *Young bulls test their strength in a pushing contest.*
**2** *An elephant will drink as much as 150 litres of water a day.*

# Lonely Bulls

LONE BULL ELEPHANTS, sometimes in the company of younger 'askaris', are a feature of elephant society. One famous old bull, often seen alone but sometimes accompanied by as many as 12 youngsters, was Mandleve. He's been gone for some years now; the great heart that drove his massive body for 60-odd years finally gave in somewhere in the privacy of thick thornbush. Mandleve was perhaps not as massive as some other bull elephants that have wandered through the Lowveld, but his tusks are the heaviest pair in the National Parks collection.

For years Mandleve roamed his territory in the Sand River valley and was often to be found in the Sabie Sand Private Game Reserve just to the north of Skukuza. Mostly he treated the open Land Rovers containing the reserve's guests with mild indifference, frequently allowing them to approach so closely that it seemed possible to reach out and touch the rough, deeply cracked, towering flanks. But the sense of proximity was more an illusion, heightened by Mandleve's sheer size, than of anything more daring or reckless, as the probity and good sense of the rangers driving the vehicles meant that a respectful (and safe) distance was always kept. The experience of being so close to one of the legendary bulls of the Lowveld was moving beyond description.

Mandleve and some of the other huge tuskers of the Lowveld – such as Shingwedzi, Shawu and Kambaku – were known as 'the gentle giants'. By contrast others, including Mafunyane and Ndlulamithi, did not display such equanimity, and it is probably just as well that these mean-tempered bulls favoured areas of the Kruger National Park well away from the tourist beat.

These legendary old bulls that once ruled over vast areas of the Lowveld have all passed on, but others just as impressively equipped have taken their place. The Kruger Park and adjacent private reserves are probably the only region in Africa where sightings of great male elephants with heavy ivory are almost assured.

It is not only old bull elephants that live out their lives in solitude, for lone males feature in the social structure of a number of other animal species. For example, single male wildebeest are characteristic of the Lowveld landscape, typically standing still as statues in the scant shade of a thorn tree as they wait out the heat of the day. These are not outcasts from the herd, but bulls in their reproductive prime which, despite protracted periods of inactivity, will defend their territories against rivals with great resolve and vigour. A life apart is also a feature of buffalo society; old males may leave the herd either to congregate in typically small bachelor groups or to live for the most part entirely alone.

**Right:** *Impressive ivory is not always a reliable indication of an elephant's age, and it is rather the sunken temples of this solitary bull that attest to his advanced years. Elephants can live to an age of about 65.*

**1** *A solitary buffalo bull. It is the lone males that earn the buffalo its well-deserved reputation for being one of Africa's most dangerous animals, for they are unpredictable and intolerant, and will readily charge any creature invading their space.*

**2** *Male wildebeest also tend to be solitary.*

1　2

**Left:** *A kudu bull with an impressive pair of horns. Bulls reach sexual maturity at about six years of age, but their spiral horns continue to grow for another year. The longest on record measure 181 centimetres.*

**1** *Sable antelope, with their arching, sabre-like horns and striking markings, are unmistakable. Several hundred occur in the Kruger National Park and adjacent private reserves, where they prefer open bushveld.*

**2** *A nyala bull. Sometimes confused with kudu, nyalas are much more slender animals.*

**3** *Waterbuck bulls bear a pair of deeply ridged horns.*

3

# Horns of Splendour

ITS POWERFUL BUILD and proud carriage alone would make the sable an impressive animal. Add its deep brown colour, strikingly marked with white on the face, belly and rump, and its long, backward-curving horns and it becomes a serious contender for the accolade of the Lowveld's most handsome antelope. Males and females are similar, but the males tend to be darker, almost black in older bulls, and their horns are usually much thicker.

Fair numbers of sable antelope live in the Lowveld, most of them in the Kruger National Park in areas of open veld, where they move in herds of as many as 30 individuals. Their gregarious and fairly sedentary habits, as well as their preference for the open, make sable fairly easy to spot, especially in areas where they are more abundant such as around Pretoriuskop and along the road between Phalaborwa and Letaba camp. Waterholes in these areas can be good places to 'ambush' sable, as they do need to drink at least every second day. The larger herds are mostly made up of females and their offspring, as by the time males reach three to four years of age they are evicted and move off to join bachelor herds. Older males tend to be solitary and territorial.

The sable's strong rival in the antelope elegance stakes is most certainly the kudu, especially males with their majestic, spiralled horns. Kudu are far more numerous than sable – some 4000 of them roam the Lowveld – and they are more widely distributed in small herds comprising one or two mature males with several females and juveniles. In late summer and early winter you may be lucky enough to spot really young kudu calves moving about within the maternal herd. Newly born kudu are often overlooked during a casual game drive, however, as the calving season is during February and March, a time when the grass is at its tallest.

Even adult kudu are surprisingly easy to miss, for they rely heavily on concealment as a defence and inhabit scrubby woodland, and acacia and mopane woodland, where their dun-coloured coats and striped flanks make them difficult to make out in the tangle of branches, leaves and undergrowth. One would imagine that the male kudu's impressive horns would be a hindrance in the often dense thicket, but when startled into flight he lifts his head so that the horns lie flat across his neck as he weaves expertly through the maze of trunks and boughs.

1  2

# Safety in Numbers

A HERD OF ABOUT 300 BUFFALOS – an average-sized group for the South African Lowveld – emerges from the roadside thicket, moving into full view of the occupants of a few motor vehicles that have pulled to a halt along a dusty byway to watch the spectacle. The tightly gathered mass of heavy, black bodies with lighter-coloured youngsters moving about underfoot but always close to their mothers, seems unperturbed at the human intrusion. Encapsulated in their vehicles, the visitors hold no perceived threat for the herd, but they have been noticed and closer observation shows several massive heads staring balefully towards the cars.

Most visitors will be excited enough to see buffalo, but after watching them for a few minutes will become bored and ready to move on, eager to find and tick off the next 'must-see' species. Those that do take the time to observe the herd for longer, however, will become intrigued by the interaction within it. They will soon see that it comprises any number of smaller units, and that these sub-herds are generally made up of several clans of females, each with four or five bulls in attendance.

Buffalo are highly sociable creatures and exchanges between individuals are constantly taking place. Nose-to-nose contact, licking, touching while lying down and even chin resting on a companion are all part of their ritual behaviour. Displays of aggression, dominance and submission, too, are constantly being played out.

Dominant males advertise their status by ground horning and tossing sand, and also by kneeling on their forelegs to rub their necks on the ground. Standing broadside to other males to show off their bulk to good advantage is another tactic, while head-to-head confrontation, combined with other threat displays, can mean the more serious possibility of actual combat. Physical clashes are mostly avoided, however, by the animal of lesser status simply turning away, or wheeling and running off, mouth open and bellowing loudly.

Male displays of dominance are especially common as a prelude to courtship, when bulls are particularly anxious to impress and dominate the females in the group. Courtship behaviour includes the bull licking a female in oestrus, testing her urine and resting his head on her rump. The female in turn may move away or make defensive threats before allowing the bull to mount her.

Among the more gregarious grazing and browsing animals of the African savanna, keeping up with the herd is an essential part of survival strategy. This is especially so amongst buffalo and so the time of birth is one of particular vulnerability for a female and her new-born calf. Although the young are on their feet within a few minutes of being dropped, it is a good few hours before they can follow their mothers and several weeks before they are strong enough to move at the pace of the herd.

**Above:** *African buffalos mill about on the banks of a river, looking like a herd of oversized black cattle. The buffalo is a highly gregarious animal, and herds frequently number a hundred or more individuals – some herds of over 600 have even been recorded. Yet lone buffalo are also often seen; these are likely to be old bulls which no longer have a role to play within the herd.*
**1** *Adult buffalos crowd round a youngster, ready to defend it against any adversary.*
**2** *A herd of buffalo raises a massive cloud of dust as it moves through dry scrub.*

1

**1** *The popular Tshokwane picnic site between Skukuza and Satara provides an ideal opportunity to stretch one's legs after hours of driving in the Kruger Park.*
**2** *A chacma baboon clutches a discarded beer can. Monkeys and baboons have learned that camps and picnic sites offer rich and easy pickings.*
**3** *A sighting beyond compare. A huge elephant bull brings traffic to a standstill.*

2    3

# *Encounters with Game*

YOU COULD BE FORGIVEN for momentarily being lulled into thinking you are anywhere but in one of the greatest game reserves on our planet. The road is tarred and well maintained, and you are pottering along within the speed limit of 50 kilometres an hour. You have long stopped jerking to a sudden halt and reversing to examine yet another dead log artfully disguised as a sleeping lion, or a large grey boulder that definitely moved and looked for all the world like the rear end of a rhino. It is hot and you begin to feel the restlessness of your companions. An ice-cold beer back at the camp is a growing imperative. Where is all the game?

Then, as you crest a low rise and lazily round a slight bend, no more than a few hundred metres ahead stands a female elephant browsing at the roadside. Cautiously you edge nearer until you are as close as good sense allows. It is tempting, but probably foolish, to switch off the engine to catch the sound of her snapping off small leafy branches with her trunk. Any vestige of boredom within the car is gone in an instant,

all eyes fixed on the huge mammal patiently going about her business.

So absorbed are you and your fellow game-viewers that at first you don't notice the other elephants moving just beyond the first curtain of bush. But then the matriarch stops to gaze fixedly at your car. Her trunk lifts slightly in your direction, testing the air. It was not your wish, perhaps, but nonetheless in your eagerness for a closer look, you have disturbed her. She gives an unseen signal and starts across the road in front of you. From out of the bush behind emerge some 20 other elephants – mature females, boisterous youngsters and babies not yet in control of their trunks. Obediently they follow her lead and within a minute or two they are lost to sight, absorbed by the thick bush on the far side of the road.

The car is quiet. Its occupants all know that if not another single animal is seen for the rest of the day, they have been privy to one of the great sights of the African wilderness.

**Above:** *A party of tourists encounter a white rhino, but one of them rather stupidly leans well out of the window to get 'that shot'. One of the great pleasures of touring the byways of the Kruger Park is the unpredictability: hours can pass with little excitement and then, around the corner, the experience of a lifetime can unfold.*
**4** *A group of ground hornbills foraging at the roadside is worth stopping for and quietly observing.*
**5** *Night drives in the Kruger Park are a relatively recent innovation. The game-drive trucks leave the camp in the late evening and will return well after dark.*

4  5

*1 Black-collared barbets are great favourites among the birds that frequent the camps in the Kruger Park. The melodic duets between the male and female ring out as they perch prominently, bobbing up and down and opening and closing their wings as part of the entertaining concert.*
*2 The immaculately kept surrounds and typical rondavel accommodation of Letaba camp.*

1  2

# Camp Life

AS YOU DRIVE through the main gates at Skukuza, the 'capital' of the Kruger National Park, you have the distinct impression of entering a well laid-out, medium-sized town. On your way to the reception area you pass a petrol station and garage, a post office and a bank. Further on, a large complex on the banks of the Sabie River comprises a small, but well-stocked supermarket, a restaurant and a fast-food outlet. All around, beautifully tended lawns and flowerbeds flourish in the dappled light filtering through the canopy of magnificent trees – giant, sprawling sycamore figs, ramrod-straight knobthorns, fever trees.

'Intimate' hardly describes Skukuza or the other main camps in the Park, but some of the older-style camps, such as the much smaller Punda Maria, do have a certain charm. For visitors wanting to be a little away from the bustle of the larger camps, there are alternatives: bushveld camps, to which access is limited to overnighting guests, and 'private camps' that are booked out to a single party, are dotted throughout the Park. Some, such as the delightful Boulders Camp set on the slopes of a rocky outcrop and surrounded by seringa trees and stately baobabs, are well away from the beaten track. Others, such as Jakkalsbessie next to Skukuza, combine privacy with the convenience of a main camp close at hand.

The Kruger Park offers visitors a wide range of accommodation, from furnished tents and huts with ablution facilities nearby, to huts with showers and toilets *en suite* and self-contained family cottages. At the top of the accommodation options there are also a number of so-called 'donor' houses, some more luxurious than others, but all extremely comfortable. Built with funding from individuals and organisations, these houses are essentially 'private', although for a certain number of nights a year they are made available to the general public. Often set in their own enclosed gardens and tended by an attentive staff, donor houses are not a bad option if you are travelling with a small group of friends and are prepared to pay modestly over the odds for additional privacy.

And in some of the camps, you don't even have to leave the gate to enjoy excellent game-viewing opportunities. At Skukuza you can idle away an hour or two on a bench overlooking the Sabie River, watching the resident crocodiles and hippos and the transient visitors: elephant, lion, buffalo, leopard, bushbuck, monkeys and baboons – they all come down to drink at some stage. A superb camp for general game-viewing is Olifants, high on the scarp above the river of the same name. Here you can see for miles across the valley, and a morning or afternoon's 'watch' with the help of a good pair of binoculars can be very rewarding.

Relaxing around the camp also allows time for noticing the smaller creatures that are often missed or ignored while out on a drive. A chameleon labouring determinedly along a branch, maybe, or a troop of vervet monkeys passing through. Beware the monkeys, though, for they'll be watching you even more closely, alert to that moment when your attention is elsewhere and they can execute a lightning raid on your food supply.

3

4

1

# At the Waterhole

SLOWLY, A LONE MALE GIRAFFE approaches the waterhole. He is obviously nervous and reluctant to leave the protection of the sparse bush, and uses his advantage of height to scan the surrounding landscape. He moves in, but caution prevails and he stops for another security check. A few more steps, and then a few more.

Now the giraffe is little more than a metre or two from the water, but still he is cautious and for a moment he appears edgy enough to flee. Is he aware of a danger hidden to the fringe of car-bound watchers at the waterhole? Apparently not, for then he moves right to the shore of the muddy pool. With painfully slow progress he widens his stance until almost doing the splits, and then his head begins to dip, borne towards the life-giving liquid on a long, muscular neck.

No sooner do the giraffe's lips touch the water than he rears up, casting a great arc of droplets as he does so. He looks around and then, slowly, the head dips once more. This time he drinks more fully – but not for long, and soon he is striding away.

For most grazing and browsing animals, coming down to the water's edge increases their vulnerability. Their general strategy, therefore, is to move in warily, drink quickly and then move rapidly away, back into the relative safety of the bush. Not only does this predator-avoiding tactic make sense, it also helps to alleviate what could quickly become a veritable traffic jam of animals queuing to drink.

Other species seem not to feel any pressure to move in and out. But these are the big guns – elephant, rhino and buffalo. Aware of their relative invulnerability, they can be downright pushy in their reluctance to share the precious commodity and see off the competition with blustering shows of impatience.

2    3

# Waterbirds

AREAS OF WATER are always great places to watch birds and the waterways of the Lowveld, literally green corridors of tall evergreen trees, dense understorey and reedy banks, provide a rich habitat for a considerable number of species. Small, secretive warblers, crakes and bitterns and the brilliantly coloured Narina trogon – limited to the Pafuri region of the far north and a few records on the Sabie River – are just a few of the more elusive species that patient birders may catch a glimpse of. Other birds are bolder: egrets and herons patrolling the dam or river banks, or fish eagles perched on their high lookouts.

Most of the pans in the Lowveld are ephemeral and soon lose their water with the onset of winter. They usually do not generate the sort of habitat that supports prolific bird life, but at times they can be good places to observe migratory waders such as the wood sandpiper, greenshank and ruff. A green sandpiper, ringed plover or Caspian plover may even be seen at a pan, although they are very rare summer visitors.

The man-made dams, on the other hand, are superb all-year spots for birding. At Lower Sabie camp, for instance, there are two dams in the immediate vicinity. One, right in front of the camp, has an overflow area that is a good place to see goliath and other herons, especially the green-backed. The second dam, a little to the west of the camp, offers regular sightings of storks – saddle-billed, woolly-necked, open-billed and yellow-billed. Diligent birdwatchers may be rewarded with sightings of white-crowned plovers at the nearby Nwatimhiri causeway, the only known location for them south of the Olifants River.

Other good waterbird sites include the Kanniedood Dam at Shingwedzi camp, and Letaba camp which, although in the middle of relatively bird-scarce mopane country, lies near the Olifants and Letaba rivers, as well as the Engelhard and Mingerhout dams. Engelhard Dam is known to have hosted breeding red-winged pratincoles, while the forest fringe along the Letaba River has even provided a sighting of a bat hawk.

1 *It is evening, and cattle egrets mass over thick reedbeds after spending much of the day gleaning insects in open grassland areas.*
2 *The lesser moorhen can be confused with the larger and far more common moorhen, but the bill – nearly all yellow – and the orange to yellowish green legs are reliable clues for accurate identification.*
3 *A white-faced duck, a common resident throughout the Lowveld.*
4 *Success! An exquisitely coloured malachite kingfisher alights with its prize.*

**Above:** *In a blur of wings, a flock of white pelicans performs a stately fly-past.*
5 *A grey heron stalks through the shallows. The bird's patience is impressive as it waits, all movement frozen, for the right moment to strike at prey with its strong, sharply pointed bill. Occasionally a grey heron might dive for a fish from a vantage point, submerging completely in the process.*
6 *A sighting of a white-backed night heron is uncommon to rare in southern Africa, especially as this heron is predominantly nocturnal in habit.*

2

3

4

5　6

# Troop Life

AFRICA IS HOME to more than half the Old World monkeys known, but most of them live in the rainforests of equatorial Africa, largely hidden from man. In the South African bush only three species are found, and of these only the vervet monkey and the chacma baboon are common. The third, the samango monkey, is an inhabitant of dense gallery and riverine forest and seldom appears in more open savanna habitats.

Both the vervet monkey and the baboon are highly sociable animals, with a baboon troop having one of the most complex social systems of any animal. Dominance, male–female and male–male alliances, emigration and immigration all play a significant role. In addition, these primates' systems of communication, vocal and otherwise, almost match those of the great apes in their variation and subtlety. They span communication between members of the same troop and between other troops, with which there is often fierce competition for resources. At the base of baboon society, however, is the fact that within the troop there is constant interplay aimed at achieving and maintaining dominance. Also, it is known that rank is largely inherited; for example, the offspring of a high-ranking female inherit her status. It is a strict and stable system and, although there may be minor changes in the status of young females, from the age of about two-and-a-half years (before sexual maturity is attained, at about five years) a female's rank is set for life.

The only time that dominance rivalries among baboons are suspended is when the troop is confronted by a common threat such as a predator, or when there is a border dispute with a neighbouring troop. Baboon males will close ranks to face the threat with a united front, and this is one of the reasons why baboon troops can roam the bush with impunity, even when a pride of lions is in the vicinity. The larger predators act opportunistically and are quick to attack any laggards, but seldom will they confront a troop head-on. With fearsome canines set in powerful jaws and a solid, stocky build, a single, fully grown male baboon is formidable in his own right, and in concert a number of males form a fighting unit not to be trifled with.

1

**1** *Young baboons play-fighting. Baboons are highly social animals, and in all troops there is a definite pecking order. Skirmishes are common in baboon society as individuals test their strength and establish dominance.*

**2** *Vervet monkeys, too, are social and move around in troops of 30 or more individuals. Unlike baboons, which spend much of their time foraging on the ground, vervet monkeys are skilled climbers and largely arboreal in habit.*

2

3    4

**Above:** *A troop of baboons relaxes on a dirt track, many of them partaking in mutual grooming sessions. Close by, but generally feeding and roaming on the outskirts of the troop, will be a number of large, aggressive male baboons. These are the guards, always at the ready to warn their companions of possible danger.*

**3** *The baboon's diet is wide and varied, but mostly comprises berries, insects and succulent new shoots. Bulbs and roots, birds' eggs and fruits are also eaten.*

**4** *A young baboon rides 'piggy-back' on its mother.*

2 *Unchecked hunting in the Lowveld in the closing years of the nineteenth century saw the white rhino plummet to extinction there. Re-introduced in the 1960s, white rhinos now number more than 2000.*

3 *Unlike the lion that seems doomed to an existence only within protected game areas, the leopard is more adaptable. Its solitary, secretive nature and eclectic diet ensure a much wider distribution.*

4 *Elephants are essentially unaggressive, but they have been known to kill humans whom they have perceived as a threat. Contests between young male members of a herd are to establish dominance hierarchy.*

## The Big Five

**Left:** *A lone buffalo bull stares balefully at the camera. For big game hunters, the buffalo is one of the most respected of all animals. And with great justification, for males – weighing up to 850 kilograms – are mean-tempered at the best of times and extremely dangerous if cornered or wounded.*
**1** *A mature male lion, undisputed as the most powerful carnivore in Africa.*

LION, LEOPARD, ELEPHANT, buffalo, rhino … the names evoke excitement, awe, a sense of danger. These are the 'big five' that present the greatest challenge to hunters. The Lowveld is still home to a number of hunting ranches, but by far the greatest number of 'hunters' that visit the Lowveld these days are more intent on shooting their quarry with cameras.

Although the emphasis has moved from killing these majestic species to simply enjoying the wonder of seeing them, in no way does it diminish the thrill of the experience. By any standards, these are impressive animals, each one dangerous in the extreme. The African bush abounds with tales of encounters with them, many of which have ended in tragedy. Even today, the big five remain a real threat to rangers, researchers and maintenance staff working in the field. Old bull buffalos, in particular, are notoriously irascible, as are black rhinos. Lions and leopards, despite their fearsome reputations, are generally less likely to attack humans, but females with young and old individuals past their hunting prime are always treated with great caution.

Over the years there have been innumerable fatal and near-fatal human encounters with the big five. Some of these stories have become legend, but most are hardly documented outside the reports of the individuals concerned in the dramas. As recently as 1997, a field ranger was attacked and badly mauled by a lion. His life was saved only by the quick thinking of his colleague, who kept his nerve and waited for the clear shot with which he killed the lion. In two incidents the following year, the victims were not so fortunate. A group of rangers moving through thick bush was set upon by an elephant that killed one of the party before his companions could come to his aid. And then, a ranger leading a game drive was attacked and killed by an old leopard that came at him from a deep culvert near a bridge in the extreme south of the Kruger Park.

3  4

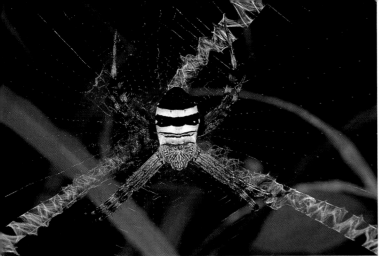

1, 2

3

**1** *Female golden orb-web spiders build massive webs suspended between the boughs of trees. The male spiders are tiny compared with the females, and spend their lives on the fringes of the web. For them mating is a dangerous game, and even if they effect copulation there is a good chance that they will be caught and eaten by the female before they can escape.*
**2** *The large-spotted genet is an agile and successful night-time hunter.*
**3** *A water monitor hunts for beetles in rhino dung.*

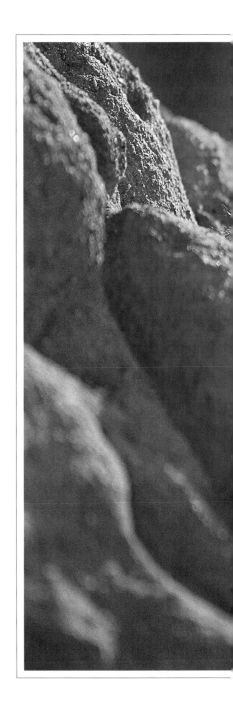

# *Attention to Detail*

NOTHING IS HAPPENING down at the river. Every tall nyala and jackal-berry tree has been scanned for the leopard that must be lying up somewhere on some stout branch, hidden by foliage and dappled light. At ground level, the massed wispy stems of *Phragmites* reeds wave pliantly in the breeze. And beyond, the water moves sluggishly under the Lowveld sun, dividing here and there to eddy round the occasional smoothly worn, grey boulder.

It is a restful scene, but soon the expectant game-viewers grow restless and eager to move on in search of action. Then someone notices a small movement on a bare branch overhanging the water. A flicker, just enough to catch the eye. Binoculars are focussed and there in sharp relief is a large water monitor, its mottled grey skin almost the colour of the branch it is lying on.

Experiences such as this simply serve to reinforce the fact that in the overriding quest for sightings of the big and bold, the smaller, less obvious creatures of the Lowveld are so often missed. No matter how quiet the bush may seem, there is always something somewhere that is going on, and all that is needed to witness it is a keen eye and patience.

Watching the smaller creatures of the bush can be hugely exciting and rewarding in its own right. For example, just by stopping to observe a giant land snail crossing the road, you may well catch a glimpse of another creature scuttling through the grassy verge, or a leopard tortoise labouring across the veld. While pausing to admire the handicraft of an orb-web spider, the strands of its trap bejewelled with droplets of dew, you may be fortunate enough to see a colony of dwarf mongooses emerge from their refuge in a nearby disused termite mound, or perhaps the silvery back of a honey badger as it makes its way home after a night of foraging.

And, of course, as you allow yourself to be drawn into the minutiae of Lowveld life, there is always the chance that some bigger, bolder drama will unfold before your eyes.

**Above:** *Often it is the smaller animals of the Lowveld that provide unexpected game-viewing highlights. Taking the time to stop and watch the activities of a pack of dwarf mongooses will seldom disappoint. They are engaging little animals, highly social and hierarchical, and their antics are most entertaining.*
**4** *The leopard tortoise is the common tortoise of the Lowveld.*
**5** *The porcupine is a large, robust rodent that can reach a weight of some 24 kilograms and can live for up to 20 years.*

4   5

1   2

3

**Below:** *The cheetah does not have a pride system like the lion's, nor is it solitary like other cats. Cheetah are sighted mostly in groups of two or three individuals – a female and her offspring, or sometimes males that are known to bond in lasting alliances, jointly defending their shared territory.*

**1** *Cheetah mark their territories and regular routes by spraying, defecating and sometimes claw-marking.*

**2** *A cheetah at its kill. Once an animal has been brought down, the cheetah loses no time in eating as much, and as quickly, as possible, as the chances are that it will be robbed by more powerful competitors, especially hyaenas.*

**3** *The fastest of all mammals in top gear, eyes fixed on its quarry and tail outstretched for balance.*

# The Daytime Hunter

THE CHEETAH OF TODAY is the last in a line of sprinting cats, fossil records of which reveal at least four species. One of these was lion-sized and roamed the steppes of eastern Europe some 500 000 years ago. The cheetah is also the most specialised of Africa's big predators, lacking both the versatility of the leopard – which easily adapts to any habitat other than true desert and can live off anything from rodents and small birds to large antelope – and the power of lions and spotted hyaenas. Both the latter also have the advantage of living in groups. Instead, for the cheetah to survive it must have open savanna with a ready supply of medium-sized antelope for prey.

The cheetah's habitat and food requirements have placed it in head-on conflict with livestock farmers, and today few of these graceful cats live outside protected areas. The only real exception to this is in Namibia, which is inhabited by about 3000 individuals – the largest population of any African country, and about 95 per cent of which is still able to exist outside conservation areas. Even so, this is a sad situation for a country that during the past 15 years has lost as many as 10 000 cheetah.

In the Lowveld there are no more than 200 cheetah, but their preference for open country and their daytime lifestyle means that they are still regularly seen. The Lowveld is also home to an interesting variant, the king cheetah, of which most individuals occur in the south-central area of the Kruger Park. When this variant was first described, in 1927 from a skin that originated in what was then Rhodesia, the king cheetah was supposed to represent a separate species. Indeed, its rich black stripes and mottled markings make it appear very different from the normal spotted form, but the king is every bit the same species. Its extraordinarily patterned appearance is now known to be the result of a recessive gene.

Lions rely on their great power to bring down prey, while leopards use the strategy of stealth followed by a pounce. The cheetah, on the other hand, relies solely on its speed to overtake and bring down its quarry. Its top speed – an incredible 112 kilometres an hour – and awesome acceleration are more than a match for even the fleetest antelope, but it can't keep up a chase for long. Within a hundred metres or so, rising temperature and oxygen debt cause the hunter to give up.

1 3

# The Russet Sea

HERE AND THERE, like the fingers on some giant hand, a baobab thrusts its branches above the surrounding landscape. Apart from the odd koppie and low ridge, these magnificent trees are the only interruptions in what is otherwise a featureless mix of yellow, red and brown. It is autumn in the northern Lowveld, and everywhere the leaves of the mopane trees are turning and beginning to fall.

The mopane is so abundant that it dominates the vegetation of some 50 per cent of the Kruger National Park, sometimes growing almost to the exclusion of other species. This might make for a very monotonous landscape, but because the mopane is so prolific, and nutritious, it is a most important food plant and a favourite of many browsers, including elephants and, outside the conservation areas, of domestic livestock too. In yet another example of the interdependence of living creatures, the taste of mopane foliage is apparently enhanced by a small, cicada-like insect that lives on the leaves at certain times of the year. Its larvae secrete protective waxy scales that are rich in sugars and are well liked by baboons.

Another insect associated with the mopane, and far better known, is a species of emperor moth that produces a voracious and brilliantly coloured caterpillar. At certain times of the year these caterpillars, or mopane worms as they are popularly known, inundate the host trees, stripping them bare of their leaves. The gaudy larvae are rich in protein and are relished by many birds and mammals, including man.

To the rural people of the Lowveld, and indeed throughout the kingdom of the mopane which stretches well to the north and westwards into Botswana and beyond, the mopane worm is regarded as a tasty delicacy, whether fresh, sun-dried or as an addition to stews. In fact, the mopane worm is the focus of a thriving industry and is even available canned in tomato or peri-peri sauce!

**Right:** *Mopane veld stretches as far as the eye can see, the landscape broken only by a gentle sweep of the Letaba River. The mopane is the dominant tree species north of the Olifants River.*
*1 The aromatic leaves, with their characteristic butterfly shape, turn yellowish gold with the advent of winter.*
*2 Mopane leaves provide a staple food for the many elephants that live in the more northern reaches of the Lowveld.*
*3 Mopane worms are the brightly coloured caterpillars of a species of emperor moth. They occur in great numbers and are an important source of protein for insect-eating animals.*

1  2

# Bush Horizons

THE LOWVELD IS NOT A PLACE of dramatic landscapes – for the most part it is flat with barely perceptible undulations. Here and there the monotony is interrupted by low, rocky ridges and granite outcrops weathered into irregular piles of massive, smoothly rounded boulders. The central grassy plains of the Kruger National Park are only about 250 metres above sea level and in the south-west, in the region from Pretoriuskop down towards Berg-en-Dal and Malelane – which is positively mountainous by Lowveld standards – the highest point is the 829-metre-high hill known as Khandzalive. Even the low rise of the Lebombo Mountains, which mark the eastern boundary of the Kruger Park, seldom exceeds 400 metres in height. The only other hilly parts of the Lowveld are towards Olifants and Letaba camps, and then again in the far north of the Park, around Punda Maria.

More often than not, any real definition to be found in the uniform sea of the Lowveld landscape is provided by tall trees that thrust their crowns proudly above the surrounding canopy. Most obvious among these is the baobab, but others, too, make their mark. The marula, for instance, with its tall, straight trunk supporting a high, rounded crown, is one of the more prominent trees of the Lowveld. It contributes far more than just its characteristic form, however, as it is one of the most important food plants of the region. The fruit, especially, is sought after by a wide range of animals that includes monkeys and baboons, elephants and many of the antelope species. Man, too, has developed a taste for the fruits that are rich in vitamin C and are used to make jams and jellies, beer and a popular cream liqueur.

Helping to sculpt the landscape and often occurring as companions to marulas are majestic leadwoods and knobthorns. The latter favour clay soils and floodplains where they can grow to almost 20 metres.

Whereas mature marula, knobthorn and leadwood trees are seldom found in stands, two other striking species of the Lowveld occur in dense groups. The silver cluster-leaf is prominent around Pretoriuskop, while north of the Olifants River the mopane grows almost to the exclusion of all other species.

Perhaps the most intriguing of the tall trees, however, is the apple-leaf, also known as a 'rain tree' because of the aphids that often infect it. These tiny insects exude a sweet foam that drips from the branches, often leaving a wet patch on the ground below.

**Above:** *The Lowveld, as the name suggests, is mostly low-lying, the undulating plains generally lacking in any dramatic land formations. Where prominent rocky outcrops do occur, such as Legogote shown here, they are important landmarks and feature widely in the journals and books of the colonial explorers of the past. For the transport riders ferrying goods between the Highveld goldfields and Delagoa Bay on the coast of what was then Portuguese East Africa, they were beacons of great significance.*
**1** *A boulder-strewn granite outcrop.*
**2** *Trees are fundamental to the character of so many Lowveld landscapes. Here a silver cluster-leaf graces the roadside. Often growing in dense stands, this species is found mostly in areas of higher rainfall, such as around Pretoriuskop.*

**3** *White seringas adorn a rocky ridge.*
**4** *The Olifants River flows through the low rise of the Lebombo range, which forms a boundary between South Africa and Mozambique.*

# *Gentle Giant versus Bad-tempered Brawler*

MUCH IS MADE of the differences between white and black rhinos – the former is often portrayed as positively amiable compared with the black rhino, which has a fearsome reputation as a cantankerous animal that will charge at the slightest provocation. There is a general truth in these observations of rhino behaviour, but far more pertinent are the very definite, and different, ecological niches that the two species have carved for themselves. The much larger white rhino is a grazer, its wide, square mouth well adapted to cropping on the short grasses it favours. The black rhino, on the other hand, is a specialist browser and has a noticeably prehensile upper lip that is used to grasp and twist off branches.

Further differences between the two species include their social behaviour. White rhino are relatively social animals in that the females and their young associate in groups. Males tend to be solitary but may be tolerant of other males within their territories, as long as the hangers-on know their place and do not try to mate with females within the territory. In the black rhino, the adults of both sexes tend to be solitary.

White rhino were once plentiful in the Lowveld, but unchecked hunting in the late nineteenth and early part of the twentieth centuries saw its demise from the region. In the early 1960s, however, a few rhinos were brought to the Kruger Park from the Umfolozi Game Reserve in what is now KwaZulu-Natal. They were released near Pretoriuskop and since that time there have been a number of other re-introductions. Today there are some 2000 white rhinos back in the Lowveld, mainly roaming in the area to the south of Skukuza.

The black rhino fared no better and by the mid-1930s it, too, had died out in the region. Again, it was re-introduced, beginning with 20 individuals brought in also from KwaZulu-Natal. Although black rhinos are not as numerous as their white cousins, their Lowveld population is increasing steadily and now amounts to more than 250 animals.

The rhinos of the Lowveld have huge significance in the struggle to conserve both species and to secure their future. Almost without exception, the few remaining populations of wild rhino in Africa are under severe threat from being poached for their horns.

**Far right:** *The white rhino, its distinctive square lips clearly shown, is considerably larger than the black rhino and has a far more equable nature than its cousin, which has a well-earned reputation as an irascible inhabitant of the bush.*

**1** *Whereas the white rhino is a specialist grazer, the black rhino is a browser, its hooked, prehensile upper lip providing an ideal tool for grasping shoots and small branches.*

1

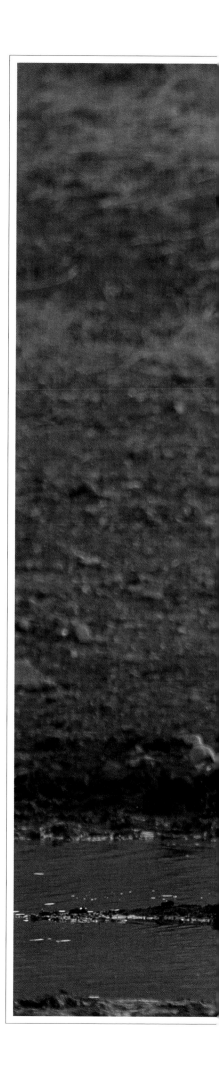

# The Promise of Rain

THERE IS A TENSION in the air towards the end of winter that is palpable. The plants and animals have made it through the worst of times and now the rains must come to revitalise the earth. To the east, over the huge expanse of water that is the Indian Ocean, the prevailing weather systems are changing and beginning to drive moisture-laden low-pressure systems down through the Mozambique Channel. At the same time, high-pressure systems push up over the landmass of the country to the south and west.

The signs are promising. At first the afternoon sky hosts only a scattering of fluffy clouds, but as the days go by so the clouds become bolder, teasing the veld with great thunderheads towering in the distance.

Still the clouds build, and now the occasional rumble of far-off thunder rolls across the veld. And then on one magical day the sky closes overhead and the first big, fat drops hit the dusty earth. One here, one there, and then faster and faster they splat down until in a triumphant climax it is pouring, with thunder and lightning crashing and flashing all around.

Few things are as exhilarating as the first real storm of summer – it is a feeling of relief, the fulfilment of a long-awaited promise, a sense of rebirth, and awe at the power and fury of nature. As thirsty as the earth is, it simply cannot absorb all the water being thrown at it from the heavens. All around little rivulets form, hesitatingly at first, then with growing confidence they find the natural slopes. Joining forces with other nascent streams, they are soon hurrying towards the nearest riverbed, already filling of its own accord.

The storm reaches a crescendo as thick columns of raw electricity arc between cloud and earth. There is no pause between the bolts of lightning and the crash of thunder; they coincide with an explosive crack that splits the air.

Then, as suddenly as it started, the storm moves on, watering the veld in its path as it cuts a swathe across the landscape. The thunder and lightning recede too, and there is silence but for dripping branches and the soft gurgle of flowing water. Everywhere the land is soaking up the moisture, while the earth and plants release a heady thanksgiving cocktail of sweet, pungent and herby aromas.

A bedraggled fork-tailed drongo flies from a temporary refuge to a nearby vantage point. An energetic bird at the best of times, this one seems especially alert. He doesn't have long to wait. The rains have triggered the emergence of thousands of winged termites from the myriad nests that honeycomb the savanna soils. In a short prenuptial flight, the insects flap about inexpertly for a while before the females settle on the ground or a grass stalk, shed their wings and give off a faint scent, or pheromone, to attract a mate. During this above-ground interlude, the termites fall easy prey to insectivorous birds such as flycatchers, bee-eaters and, of course, the drongo, which is soon swooping and swerving his way through the winged throng.

1

2

**Above:** Lightning strikes, carrying with it the promise of rain and the threat of fire. After the long, dry months of winter, the parched earth, the trees and other plants, and the animals soak up the rain, and the Lowveld is refreshed. Summer storms, welcome as they are, can be vicious affairs, turning dry riverbeds into raging floodwaters in an instant.

**1** Dark rain clouds provide a dramatic backdrop to a large knobthorn, newly in leaf and still showing its spikes of cream flowers.

**2** A female baboon huddles in the rain, doing her best to protect her baby from the heavy downpour.

3

**3** *The time after a late
afternoon storm in the
Lowveld has to be experi-
enced to be understood.
Everything is washed
and clean, for a moment
it is cooler and clearer,
and wonderful aromas
released by the plants
perfume the air.*

1    2             3

**Left:** *An impala ewe focuses intently on a perceived threat, her young lamb close at her side. Impala give birth to single young following a gestation of about 200 days. For the first few days the lamb remains hidden in a secluded spot, but soon it joins its mother as part of the herd. Despite the constant vigilance of the females, about half the young in any season are lost to predators.*

**1** *A Burchell's zebra foal suckles from its mother.*

**2** *As in the case of impala, blue wildebeest calving is a synchronised affair, with most pregnant females giving birth within the space of a few weeks. Within minutes a newly born calf is walking and is soon able to keep up with the herd, a prerequisite if it is to have any chance of survival.*

**3** *Female buffalos in their prime give birth after a gestation period of about 11 months. The mother-calf bond is extremely strong, and she will protect her offspring fiercely.*

# Lambing and Calving

NO LESS REMARKABLE than the mantle of green that clothes the Lowveld almost overnight after the first rains of summer is the sudden appearance of thousands upon thousands of newly born impala. It is almost as though the pregnant antelope have been waiting for this moment to drop their young in unison. While this is partly true, the ability of females to control the birthing season is often highly exaggerated. One of the more popular myths about impala is that females can delay the birth of their lambs by as much as a month. In fact, the timing is governed not by the onset of rains but rather by the onset of the rutting season at the end of the previous summer.

Most of the antelope, as well as other grazers such as zebras, have very specific calving and lambing seasons, a mechanism of nature that ensures an excess of food available to predators. But provided that about 50 per cent of the young of a given species survive, the herds of that species will show positive population trends.

Whereas the season for impala births centres around the early part of summer, buffalo drop their young much later, in January and February. Yet their success is related as much to the rains as is that of the impala. When times are good, as many as 80 per cent of the females in a herd will become pregnant and give birth. Predators, especially lions, will probably account for about half of the young buffalo in their first year, but overall the herd has the potential to increase its numbers. In times of drought, however, fewer than ten per cent of buffalo females will carry young, and a large proportion of those born will succumb to predation. Buffalo population dynamics are therefore strongly correlated to annual rainfall patterns, burgeoning in good seasons, remaining stable in average years and crashing when the rains fail.

An interesting observation in the social life of buffalo is that old bulls supposedly ostracised from the breeding herds often rejoin the herds at peak breeding time. They rapidly work their way up the dominance ladder to mate with the females when they come into season. A possible explanation for their success is that the older animals spend their 'bachelor' days in thick, food-rich vegetation near rivers, and are therefore physically stronger than the bulls resident in the herd.

# Season of Plenty

WITHIN A FEW SHORT weeks of the first rains the veld is showing signs of regeneration. Evergreen trees, their leaves and boughs washed clean of the dust of winter, look as new and fresh as the foliage sprouting from their deciduous neighbours. Many are in flower: wild teak, acacias such as scented thorn and knobthorn, and weeping wattle are just a few among those whose blooms range through white and cream to deep, butter yellow. Others are already bearing fruit – jacket-plums burst open to reveal their shiny red, jelly-like flesh, and bunches of ripening fruits hang from the magic guarri.

Beneath the canopies another green is spreading, as grasses take hold and begin to cover patches grazed bare during the preceding winter. Even the dry, dusty areas around waterholes take on the appearance of freshly mown lawns. The grasses may lack the majesty of trees and the bright blooms of some shrubs, but among the plants of the Lowveld they are the real workhorses. They grow faster than trees and shrubs do, and replenish themselves more rapidly. In doing so they are the mainstay not only of grazing herds, but also of smaller mammals – mice and other rodents – and birds and insects. It may seem difficult to comprehend, but insects alone possibly consume more vegetation than all other creatures combined.

Shallow pans and wallows that for months have been little more than depressions of cracked, cement-hard mud become shimmering mirrors of water. Elsewhere, oxbow lakes and still river backwaters are fringed with tall *Phragmites* reeds and covered with the floating leaves and delicate flowers – white through to pale blue – of *Nymphaea* lilies. Everywhere there is food and drink for the inhabitants of the bush.

**Left:** *The summer rains have performed their annual magic, rejuvenating the bush into a verdant parkland and bringing sustenance to browsers such as these kudu beneath a sjambok pod in flower.*
**1** *A yellow-billed stork probes the reedy shallows of an ephemeral pan.*
**2** *Water lilies painted in white and delicate pastel blues rise above a tranquil backwater of the Sabie River.*

# Index

Page numbers in **bold** indicate that the subject is a major theme; page numbers in *italic* refer to photographs.